SAILING
INTO
DISASTER

Ghost Ships and other Mysterious Shipwrecks of the Great Lakes

Constance M. Jerlecki

INLAND
EXPRESSIONS

Clinton Township, Michigan

Published by Inland Expressions

Inland Expressions
42211 Garfield Rd. #297
Clinton Township, MI. 48038

www.inlandexpressions.com

First Edition 2017

ISBN-13 978-1-939150-18-9

020317

Design by Inland Expressions

Table of Contents

Introduction

Appearing deceptively placid during periods of calm weather, the onset of adverse conditions can quickly transform the waters of the Great Lakes into some of the most treacherous on earth. As such, it is unsurprising that the first large vessel to ply these waters, the *Griffon*, disappeared into their depths on the return leg of its maiden voyage thus sparking a mystery that persists to the modern era. Unfortunately, the *Griffon* was only the first of the several thousand vessels to meet violent ends on these landlocked seas.

Of all shipwrecks, however, few have the ability to capture the imagination as those not leaving a single survivor to relate the details of a vessel's sinking. This fascination likely stretches as far back as to when humans first employed water transportation as a method to move people and goods between two points on land.

All of the maritime disasters described in this book involve ships that disappeared into the depths without leaving any survivors and, in most cases, very little evidence of their demise. Often taking place under mysterious circumstances, the majority of these vessels remain elusively hidden in their watery graves despite concerted efforts to uncover their final resting spots. As the largest and most remote of the five Great Lakes, it is unsurprising that many of the most perplexing ship disappearances in this region have occurred on Lake Superior with seven out of the twelve shipwrecks covered in this book having occurred on the body of water alone. Likewise, the cruelty visited upon Great Lakes mariners by late season storms since the earliest days of navigation on these waters is represented by the fact that over one-half of the chapters contained in the following pages relate losses that took place during the months of November and December.

With each year seeming to bring new discoveries from the depths of the inland seas, the possibility exists that the continued exploration of this shrouded world will eventually uncover the wrecks of many long lost ships that left port only to sail into an abyss of no return. Even if found, however, the ravages of time may have erased all of the evidence necessary to permit a thorough examination of the circumstances surrounding these mysterious shipwrecks. It is also highly likely that some of these missing ships will remain forever lost on the bottom of the lakes. In either case, little more can be done than to continue a process of documenting these wrecks in a manner that will allow future generations an insight into their past, any by doing so, keep the memories of these ships and those who sailed them alive.

Constance M. Jerlecki
January 2017

Chapter One
An Early Lake Superior Disappearance

A visitor to Sault Ste. Marie, Michigan during the summer of 1845 would have witnessed the almost unbelievable sight of a fleet of ships appearing to be sailing across land. A closer look would soon reveal these vessels had no sails on their masts and were in fact moving slowly along on heavy rollers to avoid the rapids in the St. Marys River created by the 21-foot difference in water levels between Lake Superior and Lake Huron. In terms of shipping, this short stretch of whitewater essentially isolated the northernmost of the five Great Lakes from its southern cousins by prohibiting the safe navigation of vessels any larger than the canoes used by local Chippewa Indians as they fished the river in much the same manner as their ancestors had for hundreds of years.

Although early commerce on Lake Superior relied upon the fur trade, the discovery of rich copper deposits near its shores during the early 1840s had awakened new interest in the region. From its close proximity to the lake, the growth of the mining industry in Michigan's Upper Peninsula stimulated the need for larger vessels to carry supplies to these remote settlements and transport the copper to ports on the lower lakes. While a handful of small schooners had graced its waters during the early nineteenth century, by the 1830s the bateau and the larger Mackinaw boats had come to dominate marine traffic on Lake Superior. To reach the lower lakes, some of the early schooners confined to Lake Superior made dangerous attempts at running the rapids on the St. Marys River. Not all of these endeavors proved successful, however, with at least two of their number, the *Discovery* and *Otter*, ending their careers as wrecks in the swirling waters.[1]

In 1835, the American Fur Trading Company bypassed the difficulties associated with the river by building the schooner *John Jacob Astor* at a location north of the rapids that is today Sault Ste. Marie's Sherman Park. This project made use of a lumber shipment brought up from Charleston, Ohio the previous year that was unloaded below the rapids and transported across land to the construction site. While proving a practical solution, it did nothing to solve the difficulty of bringing vessels from the lower lakes to Lake Superior. Four years later, workers pulled the schooner *Algonquin* out of the water south of the rapids to make a one-mile portage along the shoreline. With slow and steady progress, the 50-ton vessel made its way through the city streets on a set of rollers before being refloated some 3 ½ months later.[2]

The increasing demands of commerce eventually led to additional vessels making the overland journey to Lake Superior. During the summer of 1845, Captain John Watson brought the schooner *Merchant* to Sault Ste. Marie, Michigan. On this particular voyage, the sailing vessel carried the materials necessary to portage both itself and another company schooner, the *Ocean*, around the rapids in the St. Marys River. As the *Merchant* reached about the halfway point in its trip though the city streets, a significant event took place in the annals of Great Lakes shipping history when the steamer *Independence* arrived to make its own portage. Destined to become the first steamboat on Lake Superior, the arrival of this vessel generated considerable excitement in the northern community. A few days later, a bitter labor dispute resulted in several of the *Merchant*'s crew leaving the vessel as it sat landlocked on the moving rollers. While history remains mute on the precise cause of this disagreement, at least one of the former crewmembers managed to find employment aboard the newly arrived *Independence*.[3]

Having successfully negotiated the *Merchant* over the mile long portage, the moving crew prepared to refloat the vessel into the upper St. Marys River. With the steamer *Independence* sitting patiently nearby awaiting the opportunity to reenter its natural element, the launch hit an unexpected snag when the schooner became stuck. Coaxed the final few feet into the water after a considerable delay, the *Merchant* began its new career on Lake Superior.[4]

On June 10, 1847, two years after making the portage, the *Merchant* was paying one of its regular visits to Sault Ste. Marie as its crew prepared to depart on a voyage scheduled to begin that weekend. While going ashore in a small boat that Thursday afternoon, however, the vessel's master, Captain Robert Moore, suffered a broken leg when an oar struck a dock. Unable to take the schooner back up the lake on the upcoming trip due to

3

his injury, Moore asked Captain Robert Brown of the schooner *Swallow* to take command of the *Merchant*. Interestingly, this request came just after Captain Brown had survived an accident in the St. Marys River that occurred when a yawl in which he and a group of men were sounding out a channel for the schooner *Uncle Tom* overturned in the turbulent waters. Of the seven men aboard the small craft, only three survived the accident.[5]

Owned by Coe & Colt of Detroit, Michigan and manned by a crew of seven, the *Merchant* departed Sault Ste. Marie on Saturday, June 12, 1847, to begin making its way up the St. Marys River and across Lake Superior towards its first port of call, L'Anse, Michigan. Lying in the heart of the growing copper boom, the small community was at the base of the eastern shore of the Keweenaw Peninsula some 180 sailing miles west of Whitefish Point. In common with its assigned trade, the *Merchant* carried a cargo of general goods and mining supplies. In addition, seven passengers were also aboard. The passenger list consisted of E. Gregory and J. H. Woods of Pontiac, Michigan along with George Howard and L. C. Smith of Norwalk, Ohio all of whom were representatives of the National Mining Company and three unnamed men believed to have been lumbermen from Vermont en route to work in mills at L'Anse.[6]

Just prior to departure, a curious twist of fate of historical importance took place when the officers of the *Merchant* turned down one young man's offer to work for his passage on the basis of the ship already having a full crew. This individual proved to be sixteen year-old Peter White who later went on to play a leading role in the development of the mining industry in Michigan's Upper Peninsula through a long career involving numerous business and political pursuits.[7]

As one of only eleven vessels employed in trade on Lake Superior during the 1847 season, there is little doubt that the *Merchant*'s departure from Sault Ste. Marie that summer day attracted considerable attention among the local residents. Rounding Whitefish Point and with wind filling its sails, the schooner began heading westward across the largely uncharted lake. Apparently succumbing to a severe gale that swept across Lake Superior on the night of June 13, 1847, however, the heavily loaded *Merchant* never reached port.

In an era in which only the most rudimentary forms of communication existed in the northern reaches of Michigan, the disappearance of the *Merchant* went unnoticed for several weeks. News of the schooner's failure to arrive at L'Anse generated considerable concern for its safety at Sault Ste. Marie. Hoping to unravel the mystery surrounding his missing ship, Captain Moore left that small community aboard a schooner to conduct a search of eastern Lake Superior. Believing the *Merchant* was near Caribou Island when the storm struck, the searchers combed the waters surrounding the island in their quest for any sign of the missing schooner. Failing to find any trace of the *Merchant*, Captain Moore reluctantly abandoned his search and returned to port.[8]

With the return of the search party, all hope of finding the missing schooner and its crew evaporated among the citizens of Sault Ste. Marie. Vanishing without a trace into the depths of Lake Superior, the sudden loss of the

5

Merchant created further excitement when reports began surfacing that told of the mining agents traveling as passengers aboard the doomed ship were carrying $5,000 in coins for delivery to the mines.

Several months later, in the autumn of 1847, the 50-ton schooner *White Fish* came across the only piece of flotsam ever attributed to the *Merchant* when it recovered the lost ship's companionway door from the waters off the lake's north shore. Having floated aimlessly around in Lake Superior for a prolonged period, however, this piece of wreckage provided no clue as to the approximate whereabouts of the wreck.[9]

During the summer of 1852, newspapers across the region carried the sensational news of the *Merchant*'s possible discovery in the depths off Grand Island near Munising, Michigan. Coming five years following the schooner's disappearance, this account originated from a group of men that arrived at Sault Ste. Marie with the story of finding the top masts of a sunken vessel extending to within thirty feet of the water's surface while on a voyage in a small boat from Marquette, Michigan. Having marked the location of the wreck, the men spoke of plans to salvage the purported $5,000 worth of coins said to have been aboard the vessel when it sank. Despite receiving widespread interest at the time, this reported discovery soon faded into obscurity with no evidence of any salvage operation ever taking place.[10]

In the years following the disappearance of the *Merchant*, commerce on Lake Superior entered an era of explosive growth concurrent with the expansion of the mining industry. The opening of the first locks at Sault

Ste. Marie in June of 1855 finally removed the last barrier to opening unfettered trade between the largest of the Great Lakes and the lower lakes. While this eliminated the costly and time-consuming practice of unloading cargoes from vessels on one side of the rapids and reloading them aboard ships at the opposite end of the waterborne obstacle, it also made the unique overland movement of ships destined to operate in trades on Lake Superior no longer necessary. In time, bulk cargoes originating from ports on that body of water helped fuel the industrial and economic growth of the United States and Canada throughout the balance of the nineteenth century and well into the middle of the twentieth century. To this day, commerce on Lake Superior remains an important component in shaping the economies of both nations.

Resting somewhere beneath the same waters that today witness a procession of ships carrying millions of tons of cargo on an annual basis are the broken remains of a pioneering wooden schooner that met its end some 170 years ago. Perhaps one day an underwater explorer will uncover a set of slowly rotting timbers to discover the final resting place of the *Merchant* in the timeless depths of Lake Superior.

Chapter Two
Missing for 150 Years

Steam propulsion first came to the lakes during the 1817 season when the steamers *Ontario* and *Frontenac* entered service on Lake Ontario. At this point in the nineteenth century, the steamship represented the latest advancement in the march of human technological progress. As such, the construction of these steamers not only generated interest throughout the nation but also across the wide expanse of the Atlantic Ocean. Reporting the launch of the *Frontenac*, the November 1, 1816 edition of London, England's *The Morning Post* stated, "Her proportions strike the eye very agreeably; and good judges have pronounced this to be the best piece of naval architecture of the kind produced in America." Reflecting the public excitement generated by these vessels, festive crowds greeted the steamer *Ontario* with jubilant celebrations at every point along its inaugural trip.[1]

Beginning its maiden voyage on August 25, 1818, the *Walk-in-the-Water* became the first steam-powered vessel to ply the waters of the upper Great Lakes. Launched in May of that year, one legend tells of this ship taking its name from the story of a Native American who proclaimed, "Walks in the Water," as he watched American inventor Robert Fulton sail the steamboat

Clermont up the Hudson River in 1807. Another version, however, claims its name honored a Wyandot chief that died in 1817. Regardless of its true namesake, residents living along the shores of Lake Erie more commonly referred to this ship simply as "The Steamboat." Although the *Walk-in-the-Water* enjoyed only a brief career before its untimely demise near Buffalo, New York during the early morning hours of November 1, 1821, it, along with its predecessors, nonetheless heralded the beginning of a new era in Great Lakes commerce. While the region's shipyards continued to turn out sailing vessels throughout the following decades, steam was destined to replace sail as the primary motive power for commercial ships on the lakes by the 1880s.[2]

In 1839, Swedish inventor John Ericsson traveled to the United States in a bid to promote his screw-type propeller design. While at New York City in December of the following year, he met with a highly experienced master of lake steamers named Captain James Van Cleve. During this meeting, the two men reached an agreement in which Van Cleve would build a new vessel for Great Lakes service utilizing Ericsson's propeller. Built by Sylvester Doolittle, this ship, *Vandalia*, slipped into the water at Oswego, New York during the summer of 1841. As the first Great Lakes vessel equipped with a propeller, the 91-foot long *Vandalia* had all of its propulsion machinery placed at its stern. In keeping with a practice common with other early steamships, the vessel also carried auxiliary sails and rigging. With the fitting out of this groundbreaking ship proceeding smoothly over the next few months, the *Vandalia* ventured into Lake Ontario on its maiden voyage in November of that same year.[3]

The propeller, as such vessels were termed during this era, provided many incentives to ship owners. Featuring a more compact propulsion design, these vessels proved capable of carrying additional cargo in comparison to identically sized paddlewheel steamers. Proving popular, some 50 propellers had joined the Great Lakes fleet by 1850. Soon becoming a mainstay of inland commerce, this type of ship grew to dominate the trade with the exception of side-wheel steamers that remained popular in certain sectors of the passenger service.[4]

Eleven years after the *Vandalia* embarked upon its pioneering first voyage, a new vessel joined the growing list of steamships operating on the Great Lakes when Bidwell & Banta launched the propeller *Bay State* at Buffalo, New York. Built for the Northern Transportation Company, this 137-foot long wooden steamer entered service on that firm's routes covering a wide range of ports it had served between Ogdensburg, New York and Chicago, Illinois since its 1851 founding. Measuring 26 feet in beam, the design of the *Bay State* featured two decks, a single mast, and a gross tonnage of 372 tons.[5]

During the 1855 season, the Northern Transportation Company appointed Captain John Brown master of the *Bay State*. Born near Brockville, Ontario in 1826, Brown's family moved across the St. Lawrence River to the United States a short time later to take up residence in a handful of communities before settling at Ogdensburg, New York in March of 1839. Later that year, the future captain went on the lakes for the first time when, at the age of thirteen, he began a two-month stint aboard the schooner *Ontario*.

Returning to Ogdensburg, John Brown worked ashore for a year in a foundry and three years in the coopering trade before returning to the lakes to sail aboard a number of vessels before accepting a position with the St. Lawrence & Lake Ontario Steamship Company in 1849. Holding the post of wheelsman aboard the steamer *Northerner* for two seasons, he served in an identical capacity on the *Niagara* during the 1851 shipping season before becoming that vessel's second mate the following year.[6]

In 1853, John Brown began his long association with the Northern Transportation Company when that firm named him second mate of the steamer *Granite State*. That season saw Brown move among several vessels in the fleet. Two months after shipping out on the *Granite State*, he went on to serve as mate and pilot of the propeller *Michigan* for three months before being appointed master of the *J. W. Brooks*. After that steamer's boiler gave out just twelve days later, however, John Brown sailed aboard the propeller *Cleveland* before returning to the *Granite State*, where he remained for the balance of the season.[7]

Sailing as first mate of the *Wisconsin* during 1854, John Brown moved over to the propeller *Lady of the Lakes* at the beginning of the 1855 shipping season. His tenure aboard that vessel proved extremely brief as he only made one trip before managers at the Northern Transportation Company appointed him master of the *Bay State*, a position he was to hold throughout the majority of that vessel's ten-year operational career.[8]

Ever since human eyes first gazed upon them, the clear waters of the Great Lakes have demonstrated the ability

11

to create an optical illusion known as a Fata Morgana, or in simpler terms; a mirage. Created by certain atmospheric conditions that occur when a mass of warm air encounters a layer of denser cold air just above the surface of the water, such apparitions can display far away landmasses and objects just above the horizon. During John Brown's second year as master of the *Bay State*, his ship was involved in one such sighting on Lake Ontario in August of 1856. Appearing in contemporary publications conveying the history of shipping on the Great Lakes, this occurrence took place during a voyage from Niagara to the Genesee River when, at sunset, the crew and passengers of the propeller witnessed a mirage involving at least a dozen ships. Observers aboard the *Bay State* told of the vessels in the vision appearing inverted and in remarkable clarity against the darkening sky. Equating the sight as being similar to that of a painting on canvas, accounts of this occurrence tell of the mirage lasting until the coming of darkness.[9]

In December of that same year, the *Bay State* suffered a mechanical breakdown on Lake Ontario that, if it were not for the ingenuity of Captain John Brown, could have led to its loss. During a late season trip from Port Dalhousie, Ontario to Ogdensburg, the *Bay State* lost power about ten miles off Devil's Nose, a prominent bluff along the southern shore of the lake approximately 25 miles northwest of Rochester, New York. Having reported a broken valve stem, the engineer also informed Captain Brown that it was not possible to fabricate a replacement onboard. Sending the engineer ashore in one of the steamer's small boats to secure a replacement,

Brown attempted to sail the *Bay State* into the Genesee River. Failing in this endeavor due to a southwest wind, he dropped anchor about nine miles west of the river entrance.[10]

When the wind shifted into a full gale around midnight, Captain Brown put down a second anchor to fight the increasing waves. As the temperature dropped, the spray caused by the endless procession of waves crashing into the powerless steamer's hull began slowly depositing a layer of ice on its exposed surfaces. Before long, the added weight of the ice caused the bow to sink some eighteen inches deeper into the increasingly violent lake. When the unfortunate plight of the *Bay State* reached the propeller *Ogdensburg*, its crew attempted to steam out of harbor to render assistance. Finding the seas too rough to continue, however, the master of the steamer had no other choice but to turn back.[11]

As noon approached, Captain John Brown took matters into his own hands when he began fashioning a new valve stem. Using a kitchen stove as a forge, he managed to fabricate an improvised valve stem that permitted, at least temporarily, the restoration of power. Meanwhile, the engineer, whose boat had landed about fifteen miles west of the Genesee River before making his way to Rochester, was watching from the shoreline as the crew of the propeller struggled to get their ship underway. Witnessing a shower of sparks emanating from the vessel's stack, the engineer believed the ship had burst into flames. Fearing this is what had just occurred, he quickly informed the authorities that the *Bay State* had burned and sank with all hands.[12]

Fortunately, the panicked account of disaster given by the engineer proved inaccurate as the substitute valve stem managed to allow Captain Brown to sail the steamer into the Genesee River. Riding into nearby Rochester by carriage, he telegraphed the vessel's agents at Oswego to inform them that, despite earlier reports to the contrary, the *Bay State* had arrived safely in port.[13]

Remaining master of the *Bay State* throughout 1857, Captain Brown moved over to the propeller *Vermont* the following shipping season. Returning to the *Bay State* in 1859, he was to sail that vessel for the next three years. On September 23, 1862, newspapers across the northern states printed the preliminary text of the Emancipation Proclamation issued the previous day by President Abraham Lincoln alongside the latest reports emerging from the bloody battlefields of the ongoing Civil War. That same day, Captain John Brown turned over command of the *Bay State* to Captain William Marshall of French Creek, New York. After completing this task, Brown went to Cleveland to assume command of the propeller *Maine*.[14]

While visiting a shipyard at Cleveland during mid-October, Captain Marshall ran into Captain Ebenezer Elliot, an old acquaintance with several years of sailing experience. Captain Elliot had commanded many vessels during the course of his nearly twenty-year career, among which included the steamers *Boston*, *Champlain*, and *Vermont* of the Northern Transportation Company. After becoming seriously ill earlier that spring, Elliot had secured a position at the shipyard after deciding to give up working on the lakes. Presented with a promise to command the *Bay State* the following season, however, his old shipmate soon convinced him to join the ship's crew as first mate. Sailing out of Cleveland a short time later, the two friends could have no idea that disaster awaited both of them just a few weeks ahead.[15]

At 11 o'clock in the evening of November 2, 1862, Captain Marshall guided the *Bay State* out of Oswego and into the darkness of an autumn night on Lake Ontario. On this particular voyage, the steamer was carrying a cargo of general merchandise bound for delivery to Cleveland and Toledo. In addition, the vessel had taken on seven passengers. Perhaps due to the lateness of the season, this small group represented a number considerably lower than the normal passenger load carried by the *Bay State* that season. The passenger list included a resident of Vermont named Orley Thompson, who was also the nephew of John H. Crawford, an agent of the Northern Transportation Company at Oswego. The remaining travelers consisted of a woman with the last name of Scruton and her infant child, and four other persons who had secured passage in steerage.[16]

A few hours later, the weather took a deadly turn when the strong winds from the west grew into a heavy gale. Having already wreaked havoc on Lake Erie just hours before, the ferocious weather system swept across Lake Ontario. As if wiped from existence by the merciless storm that night, the *Bay State* joined the list of ships to have simply "sailed away" when it vanished into the quiet depths of the lake.

The residents of Oswego and the surrounding area did not have to wait long to begin learning the level of the devastation dealt upon maritime commerce by the storm. Carrying a mixed cargo of barley, rye, and wheat from Canada, the schooner *Annie Moulton* went ashore near Sandy Creek after losing its sails off the city. Meanwhile, the wind and waves pushed the schooner *Gazette* into shallow water to go aground about a half-mile east of the harbor entrance while carrying a cargo of lumber. On the morning following the storm, the waters of Lake Ontario surrendered the first evidence of an even larger disaster when pieces of the *Bay State* and its cargo began washing ashore a few miles west of the city.[17]

Based on sketchy information, initial reports of the *Bay State* sinking named Captain John Brown as being in command of the propeller during its fateful final voyage. Although subsequent reports from Oswego quickly revised early estimates of forty to fifty passengers being lost in the disaster downward to a more accurate figure, it was not until November 4 that regional newspapers began correctly reporting Captain William Marshall as being the master of the sunken steamer.[18]

The abundance of merchandise floating ashore from the wreck of the *Bay State* fueled a temporary windfall for local beachcombers, some of which hauled away goods by the cartful. A stretch of shoreline three miles west of Oswego provided mute testimony of the disaster by yielding a lifeboat and several official papers from the lost vessel.[19]

With no accurate record existing as to the size of its crew, establishing a definitive count of the lives lost when the *Bay State* plunged to the bottom represents an impossible task. Contemporary accounts provide estimates of the vessel's complement as ranging from sixteen to eighteen crewmembers. Combined with the seven passengers known to have secured passage on the ill-fated steamer, it is reasonable to assume that at least twenty-three to twenty-five persons lost their lives in the sinking.[20]

Certainly not ranking as one of the most significant losses to occur on the Great Lakes in terms of lives or property lost and quickly overshadowed by events occurring during the turbulent years of the Civil War, the demise of the *Bay State* soon faded into history. At the time of its loss, the propeller was valued at approximately $16,000, while its cargo likely consisted of between $20,000 and $30,000 worth of merchandise.[21]

During an era in which the annual parade of commerce on the Great Lakes normally conducts itself without suffering any disastrous loss it can be difficult to comprehend the hazards once faced on these waters by earlier generations. In the case of the *Bay State*, its sinking represented just one of the some 300 accidents to occur across the lakes during 1862 that together took 154 lives.[22]

During the summer of 2015, a team of shipwreck hunters came across the wreck of the *Bay State* lying on the bottom about 7 miles off Fair Haven, New York and 12 miles west of Oswego. Although nearly 153 years of resting on the bottom had long erased any visible trace of the vessel's name, identification of the hulk was simplified by the fact that no other propeller driven steamer of its size is known to have been lost in that section of Lake Ontario. A survey of the surrounding bottom revealed a trail of debris extending for about a

17

quarter-mile to the west of the wreck. While this discovery suggests that heavy seas began tearing away the upper works of the vessel before it sank to the bottom it also implies that Captain Marshall had reversed course to the east in an apparent bid to reach the safety of Oswego. Resting several hundred feet down, further expeditions to wreck of the *Bay State* may yet provide important clues as to its demise.[23]

Chapter Three
The Flying Dutchman of the Inland Seas

As far back as the 17th century, tales of a ship condemned to sail endlessly with no hope of ever reaching port began circulating in waterfront taverns around the globe. As the years marched on, overactive imaginations spawned several versions of this popular maritime myth. Incorporating all of the major elements of this legend, one rendition tells of a Dutch sea captain named Vanderdecken who defied a ghostly apparition appearing on the deck of his man-of-war, *Flying Dutchman,* at the height of a deadly storm during an attempt to round the Cape of Good Hope at the southern tip of Africa. Ignoring the desperate pleas of his crew and passengers along with the demands of the mystical visitor to turn back, the captain burst into a tirade of impious remarks directed at God. Angered by the display of insolent behavior, the spectral entity condemned Vanderdecken to sail the ocean for eternity aboard his cursed ship before disappearing along with the crew and passengers. From that day, the legend says, any ship sighting the *Flying Dutchman* risked suffering some form of catastrophe ranging from food provisions going bad to foundering with all hands. Usually said to take place during periods of dense fog or heavy storms, sightings often described an unearthly glow surrounding the cursed vessel even as it sailed directly into the wind with full sails.

With waters as deadly as those of any ocean, it is unsurprising that a tale similar to that of the *Flying Dutchman* was to become an enduring component of Great Lakes folklore. Despite some similarities, however, the freshwater version differs significantly from its saltwater cousin as sightings of the ghost ship did not herald some imminent calamity nor did the tale originate from the actions of some belligerent ship captain but rather an unexplained disappearance of a merchant ship at the dawn of the twentieth century.

This story begins far away from the Great Lakes at a place far more familiar with the tale of the *Flying Dutchman*, where, along the banks of the River Tees at Middlesbrough, England, the Sir R. Dixon & Company built a steel steamer for the Montreal Transportation Company in 1893. Named for the battle that secured Scottish independence from England in the year 1314, the *Bannockburn* measured 256 feet 3 inches in length, which along with a 40-foot beam and 21-foot depth permitted it to pass through the Canadian locks connecting the Great Lakes with the Atlantic Ocean. Its construction completed, this canal type vessel departed Britain by sailing into the North Sea on the first leg of a long journey across the Atlantic. Reaching Canada, the owners of this steamer immediately put it to work in the grain trade.

For the next nine seasons, the *Bannockburn* operated faithfully for the Montreal Transportation Company as it carried payloads from the upper Great Lakes to ports on the lower lakes and St. Lawrence River. With grain encompassing the majority of this vessel's annual tonnage commitments, many of these cargoes came aboard at the twin cities of Fort William and Port Arthur, Ontario located at the head of Lake Superior. During this time, the British built ship managed to avoid many of the dangers commercial vessels operating on the lakes risked during this period. Modern navigational aids such as radar and radio direction finders (RDF) lay far in the future.

One notable exception to an otherwise uneventful safety record thus far in its operational career took place on April 27, 1897 when the *Bannockburn* ran onto the rocks at Snake Island Light off Kingston, Ontario. Carrying 60,000 bushels of corn loaded at Toledo, Ohio and sailing at full speed, the impact opened a large hole in the steamer's bottom plates. The resultant flooding damaged a large portion of the cargo, 25,000 bushels of

This view of the *Bannockburn* making a lock passage illustrates the steamer's graceful design features.

which was unloaded onto barges before the subsequent salvage operation succeeded in refloating the stranded vessel.[1]

Paying one of its many visits to the Canadian Lakehead, November 13, 1902 would find the *Bannockburn* once again under the loading spouts at Fort William. On this particular occasion, the Montreal Transportation Company had assigned this vessel to load 75,000 bushels of wheat for delivery to Midland, Ontario on Georgian Bay. Continuing their work in much the same manner as done during previous loadings, the crew of the steel steamer had no clue that this was to be their ship's second to last cargo.[2]

With Kingston as its registered homeport, it is unsurprising that over half of the crew aboard the *Bannockburn* called that community at the eastern end of Lake Ontario home. Reflecting the youthfulness of its crew, the ship's complement consisted primarily of young men in their early twenties with some as young as sixteen. At age thirty-seven, Captain George R. Wood of Port Dalhousie, Ontario was nearing the completion of his first season as master of the 256-foot long steamer after having served aboard another of the fleet's vessels the previous season.[3]

Even as wheat poured into the *Bannockburn*'s cargo holds, the notoriously poor weather of November was making its presence known across the Great Lakes region. Arriving in port at 3 o'clock that afternoon, Captain James McAllister of the package freight and passenger steamer *Alberta* reported encountering heavy seas and snowstorms on Lakes Huron and Superior. Describing the weather conditions as "about the severest storm" experienced yet that season, McAllister told of having to sail the *Alberta*, one of the first two steel-hulled vessels on the lakes, along the north shore of the lake after passing Michipicoten. Interestingly, that day's port report also lists Algoma Central Steamship Company's *Leafield* as scheduled to arrive at Fort William later that evening. Built in England one year earlier than the *Bannockburn*, this ill-fated ship was to be one of two ships lost with all hands on Lake Superior during the Great Storm of 1913.[4]

Following an uneventful trip, the *Bannockburn* delivered its wheat cargo to Midland before returning up the lakes. After sailing across Georgian Bay, the steamer headed northward on Lake Huron toward the St. Marys River and Sault Ste. Marie, Ontario. Continuing up the St. Marys River after locking through at the Canadian Soo during the early hours of November 19, 1902, the *Bannockburn* passed the Point Iroquois Lighthouse on the Michigan shore as it approached the wider expanse of Whitefish Bay. Reaching Whitefish Point after steaming nearly another 25 miles, Captain Wood ordered a northwest turn to place his ship on a course that would take it across Lake Superior to the Canadian Lakehead.[5]

Completing its voyage across the frigid waters of the largest of the five Great Lakes, the *Bannockburn* tied up at the Canadian Northern Elevator at Port Arthur, Ontario on November 20, 1902. With the fall grain rush in full swing as shippers worked to move the season's final cargoes, the elevators at the twin Canadian ports bustled with activity. With heavy traffic filling the harbor, the *Bannockburn* loaded 85,000 bushels of wheat for a return trip to Midland while the steamers *Chili* and *Saturn* also took aboard grain cargoes at the same dock.

With the last grains of wheat trickling into the *Bannockburn*'s cargo hold on the morning of November 21, the deck crew began securing the ship's hatches in preparation for departure. Casting off its lines for the final time, the steamer pulled slowly away from the Canadian Northern Elevator on what for all practical purposes seemed like an ordinary late season run. The trip had barely begun, however, when the *Bannockburn* ran aground while attempting to leave harbor. Successful in freeing his ship from the bottom with no apparent damage, Captain Wood wasted little time in steaming out of Port Arthur and into Lake Superior at around 9 o'clock that windswept morning.[6]

While the *Bannockburn* began its downbound trip, the steamer *Algonquin* was making its way westward across Lake Superior toward the Canadian Lakehead. In common with most other steel vessels operating for Canadian fleets at the turn of the century, the construction of this vessel, like that of the *Bannockburn*, took place far away from the lakes in the British Isles. Built at Glasgow, Scotland in 1888 and commanded by Captain James McMaugh, the *Algonquin* operated for the St. Lawrence & Chicago Steam Navigation Company. With the ability of operating through the Canadian canals of the era representing an overriding design consideration, both of these ships, by necessity, shared many similar characteristics, including nearly identical dimensions.

Closing rapidly from opposite directions, both ships

met during the afternoon of November 21 in choppy seas approximately 50 miles southeast of Passage Island. Although an area of haze persisted over that section of Lake Superior at the time, Captain McMaugh managed to observe the *Bannockburn* sail effortlessly past on its downbound voyage. From his position on the bridge, the shipmaster watched the steamer recede into distance over the *Algonquin*'s stern before suddenly disappearing from view a few minutes later. Although losing sight of the *Bannockburn* a little quicker than expected, Captain McMaugh, possibly influenced by the low visibility conditions, attached no particular significance to the steamer vanishing into the mist as his own vessel continued its westward voyage. Unbeknownst to the captain and officers of the *Algonquin*, they had just made the last daytime sighting of the ill-fated *Bannockburn*.

Although stiff winds had buffeted lake vessels throughout the day, just hours after the *Algonquin* passed the *Bannockburn* the weather took a sudden turn as a November gale descended upon Lake Superior. With the coming darkness also came high winds and heavy seas as the unstoppable forces of nature made their power known to all caught out on the lake.

One of the ships caught in the melee that night was the Northern Navigation Company's 340-foot long freight and passenger steamer *Huronic*. Upbound Port Arthur on its regular route between that city and Sarnia, Ontario, this vessel had just entered service in May of that same year following its construction at Collingwood, Ontario. In the darkness of that night, the crew of the steamer spotted what it believed to be the lights of the downbound *Bannockburn*. While the validity of this sighting is open to question given the prevailing weather conditions, the reputation of lake sailors being extremely knowledgeable about such matters leaves little doubt as to their ability to distinguish the indemnities of individual lake ships even at night.

At the eastern end of Lake Superior and separated by an international border running down the center of the St. Marys River sits the twin cities of Sault Ste. Marie, Michigan and Ontario. Besides sharing identical names, these communities also boast of locks capable of raising and lowering ships between Lake Superior and the 21-foot lower water level of Lake Huron. As such, ships transiting between those two bodies of water must pass through one these systems of locks to avoid rapids in the river.

Following its departure from Port Arthur, the *Bannockburn*'s next port of call was to be Sault Ste. Marie, Ontario. Continuing downbound after passing through the single Canadian Lock at that city, this ship would reach Lake Huron and then Georgian Bay before finally arriving at Midland. The *Bannockburn*, however, never reached Sault Ste. Marie or any port for that matter, for at some point following the late hours of November 21, 1902 this steel steamer and its twenty member crew had simply sailed into oblivion, thus beginning a mystery that has persisted for nearly 115 years!

During the days immediately following the disappearance, stormy conditions hampered early search efforts sparked by the *Bannockburn*'s failure to report in as expected at Sault Ste Marie on Saturday, November 22,

1902. Although some concern existed for the welfare of the crew, hopes nonetheless remained high that the steamer may have sought shelter from the storm or had stranded off some isolated shoreline.[7]

On November 25, the whaleback steamer *Frank Rockefeller* of United States Steel's giant Pittsburgh Steamship Company fleet passed through a field of wreckage in the normal shipping lane off Stannard Rock at approximately the halfway point between Port Arthur and Whitefish Point. With the seas far too rough to retrieve any of the debris or identify it as coming from the missing ship, however, the *Rockefeller*'s captain had little choice but to continue downbound for the Soo Locks. Later that same day, and with its crew unaware of the growing concern for the overdue *Bannockburn*, the *Huronic* steamed out of Port Arthur to retrace its route back to Sarnia. Passing downbound through the locks, the crew apparently did not learn of the missing vessel until docking at the end its three-day voyage.[8]

As the mystery deepened during the week following the disappearance, a number of purported sightings placing the *Bannockburn* at various places of safety began appearing in newspapers across the region. One early example published in the November 27, 1902 edition of Fort William's *Daily Times-Journal* told of the grain elevator's superintendent, Mr. Sellars, as having received word of the missing ship being at anchor off the Slate Islands in northern Lake Superior. Despite the hopeful nature of this account, the reported location, some 100 miles east of Port Arthur, was far to the north of where the *Bannockburn* and *Algonquin* met on the afternoon of

November 21, not to mention the subsequent sighting further to the east by the *Huronic* later that evening. In addition, Mr. Sellars quickly came forward to dispute this story by denying he had any information concerning the missing steamer.[9]

Upon arriving at Sault Ste. Marie, Michigan on November 28, the captain of the Canadian steamer *Strathcona* contradicted a previous rumor of the *Bannockburn* being ashore on Michipicoten Island. Reporting his observations, the shipmaster told of not finding any evidence of a stranded vessel despite brining his ship to within four miles of the island on its downbound trip.[10]

That same day, J. A. Cutley, the manager of the Montreal Transportation Company received the following short, but reassuring, message sent by George L. McCurdy, an insurance representative from Chicago involved in the search for the *Bannockburn*:

> Bannockburn on shore on mainland north of
> Michipicoten Island.
> (Signed) George L. McCurdy[11]

Having endured several days of waiting without word, the families of those aboard the now seriously overdue steamer eagerly welcomed the hopeful context of this telegram and a similar message received by L. L. Henderson at the shipping company's Kingston office. Within hours, however, George McCurdy admitted his message originated from an early report said to have come from the steamer *Germanic* that told of the

Destined to become the "*Flying Dutchman*" of Lake Superior
following its mysterious loss, the *Bannockburn* operated for the
Montreal Transportation Company throughout its entire career.

Bannockburn being ashore on the mainland, a claim
subsequently disputed by the vessel's officers.
Furthermore, the insurance man added he had no definite
information on the vessel's whereabouts. Falling like a
hammer, this revelation plunged the affected families
back into an agonizing wait for further news.[12]

Prompted by the purported *Germanic* sighting, the
underwriters chartered the Great Lakes Towing
Company's tug *Favorite* to scout the area of the reported
stranding. Departing its dock at Cheboygan, Michigan,
the *Favorite* steamed up the St. Marys River and into Lake
Superior after locking upbound at the Soo. Reaching the
search area, the tug found no trace of the *Bannockburn*
despite sailing completely around Michipicoten Island
and several miles along the mainland.[13]

Arriving at Sault Ste. Marie, Michigan on November 29, the crew of the steamer *Majestic* gave further weight to previous reports of the *Bannockburn* being ashore when it told of sighting the steamer wrecked off the lake's north shore. While not venturing close to shore, the *Majestic*'s captain described the stranded vessel to Sault Ste. Marie's *Record-Herald* as being in the lee of the shore, and therefore in no danger of breaking up as long as the wind did not shift to come off the lake.[14]

The search effort expanded when the insurers hired the tug *C. L. Boynton,* to search the waters around Caribou Island. Skippered by William Landon, the 87-foot long tug also probed the area around Michipicoten Island and the Canadian shore as the weather steadily deteriorated. Proving ultimately futile like other searches, however, the efforts of the *Boynton*'s crew turned up no clue as to the *Bannockburn*'s fate.[15]

Despite the ongoing efforts of the *Boynton* and *Favorite* as they worked their way through the search area, marine underwriters quickly began to give up all hope that the *Bannockburn* was still afloat. As early as November 27, reports from Chicago told of insurance representatives in that city expressing their growing belief that the missing ship had sank sometime after passing the *Algonquin* in Lake Superior six days earlier. Information provided by these same sources listed the insurance valuation of the *Bannockburn* and its cargo as $200,000.[16]

Following an initial spate of poor weather, conditions began to clear as the first week of the search effort came to an end. With no new word forthcoming, however, hopes for the safe discovery of the *Bannockburn* and its crew continued to diminish with each passing hour.

One item to generate a considerable amount of interest following the disappearance of the *Bannockburn* was the Canadian government's decision to discontinue the navigation beacon on Caribou Island a week before the steamer's final voyage. Located in eastern Lake Superior, Caribou Island lies near the normal sailing course between Port Arthur and Sault Ste. Marie. As such, the extinguishing of this important navigational aid represented a questionable policy that created a dangerous obstacle to late-season shipping through the area.[17]

The discontinuance of the Caribou Island light generated early speculation that the *Bannockburn* possibly stranded on the reefs surrounding the island. Despite the plausibility of this theory, the tug *Boynton* located no sign of the overdue vessel during its examination of the island and the surrounding area. In addition, the discovery of the wreckage field to the west by the *Frank Rockefeller* also cast serious doubts as to whether Caribou Island played any role in the steamer's disappearance.

With Lake Superior refusing to yield any clues as to the fate of the *Bannockburn*, the search for answers shifted to the account given by Captain McMaugh of the *Algonquin*. Recalling how the ill-fated steamer suddenly vanished from view within a few minutes after passing his ship in mid-lake on the afternoon of November 21, the shipmaster concluded it had quickly plunged to the bottom following a boiler explosion. Although other officers on the *Algonquin*'s bridge also noted the *Bannockburn*'s sudden disappearance, nobody aboard heard any sign of an explosion. Therefore, it was not until learning of the canal steamer's overdue status that the crew first realized the possible significance of its observations.[18]

Captain McMaugh's explosion theory, however, stands in direct contradiction to observations made by the crew of the *Huronic* later that night. While there is a possibility that the officers of the passenger steamer mistook the lights they believed were those of the *Bannockburn* actually belonged to another downbound vessel, it remains difficult to dismiss their sighting. By their very nature, lake sailors usually develop an uncanny ability to distinguish minute differences between individual vessels not easily apparent to outsiders. As such, there is no reason to doubt the veracity of the *Huronic* sighting.

As with many other unexplained shipping disappearances on Lake Superior, the charting of Superior Shoal in 1929 prompted speculation that the *Bannockburn* may have been a victim of the formation's underwater ridges. Although well known to local fishermen, the shoal had remained virtually unknown to lake masters as it was well off their usual navigation courses. Located at least 30 miles north of the steamer's last confirmed sighting, however, it seems unlikely the steamer would have sailed that far north in the storm.

The absence of any definitive proof also fueled theories of a structural failure causing the sudden loss of the *Bannockburn*. Much of this conjecture centered upon the possibility that a hull fracture allowed the vessel's propulsion machinery to plunge through its bottom. Nearly 2 ½ years later, this theory gained further support when workers found a steel hull plate on the bottom of the Welland Canal on March 27, 1905. Contemporary newspaper accounts attempted to tie this discovery to the unexplained sinking by declaring the *Bannockburn* as being the only steel vessel to have transited the canal up to that time. This was, in fact, untrue, however, as several such ships had made passages through the Welland Canal during the same period.[19]

The very location of the mysterious hull plate's discovery cast serious doubts as to whether it could have actually come from the *Bannockburn*. Found on the bottom of a heavily traveled waterway, it is nearly impossible to connect the steel plate to the missing steamer without some unique identifying characteristic. Moreover, with the ship's last two cargoes taking it on voyages between the Canadian Lakehead and Midland, Ontario, the plate would have to become detached at some point prior to mid-November of 1902. By necessity, such a find would have required the *Bannockburn* to be in such poor structural condition that it was losing hull plates several weeks before its eventual loss. Under such circumstances, it seems highly unlikely the ship would have remained afloat long enough to make the late season grain runs.

A more simple explanation as to how a steel hull plate wound up on the bottom of the Welland Canal derives from the method of bringing ships into the Great Lakes during this era. In the days before the expansion of the locks connecting the lakes to the Atlantic Ocean, the established practice of bringing ships built on saltwater that were too long to transit the confines of these canals involved cutting them in two and rejoining the sections after reaching Lake Erie. Instead of coming from the *Bannockburn*, could not the hull plate have more easily originated from one of these ship sections during its tow through the canal?

Perhaps the most significant, and often overlooked, factor in this sinking involves the grounding suffered by this vessel during its departure from Port Arthur. Although appearing minor in nature, the brevity of the time between this incident and the resumption of the downbound voyage indicates Captain Wood believed his ship had not sustained any serious damage. Without a thorough survey of the hull, however, the possibility exists that some hidden structural damage may have proven too much for the *Bannockburn* when it encountered the stormy conditions on Lake Superior later that day.

The *Bannockburn*'s grounding at the beginning of its final voyage recalled a previous accident during the 1900 shipping season when the steamer struck a reef in Lake Huron near Port Hope, Michigan. Freed from the bottom, the ship went to Harbor Beach, Michigan for a survey by the insurance underwriters. Although this examination revealed the hull had been "seriously strained," the owners apparently made no effort to place the ship into dry dock following the accident. The lack of a more extensive survey and any necessary repairs combined with the stranding at Port Arthur may have seriously weakened the vessel's hull. These factors led many observers to believe it possible that the *Bannockburn* broke in two when it encountered the fall storm.[20]

On December 12, 1902, three weeks to the day of the *Bannockburn* embarking on its final voyage, Captain Ben Trudell of the United States Life-Saving Service station at Grand Marais, Michigan discovered a cork life preserver bearing the vessel's name during a search of local beaches. This find proved to be the first confirmed item recovered from the lost steamer. The following day, searchers came across additional wreckage washed up on shore near the station.[21]

About 18 months following the disappearance came the discovery of an oar found under a pile of driftwood on the Michigan shore. Wrapped in a tarpaulin, the oar was marked with a series of crudely carved letters spelling out the word B-A-N-N-O-C-K-B-U-R-N. This tales takes on a bizarre twist as whoever carved the lettering reportedly colored it with human blood. Although adding another dimension to this mystery, the suspicious wrapping of the oar to protect it from the weather questions the authenticity of this discovery and points more towards it being a hoax.[22]

Had it not been for a series of ghostly sighting reports beginning in the year immediately following its loss, it is likely that the *Bannockburn* would have become just one of the many ships to have sailed away to their doom on the Great Lakes. Quickly dubbed the "Flying Dutchman" of the Great Lakes, lake sailors began telling tales of spotting the *Bannockburn* sailing serenely on storm tossed waters as it pursued an endless quest to reach port. Some tellers of these stories went so far as to claim to have spied the ghostly figure of Captain George R. Wood at the helm of his ill-fated steamer. Such sailor yarns served only to elevate the allure of this mysterious shipwreck.

Three of the ships directly linked to the tale of the *Bannockburn* went on to have widely disparate careers. The *Algonquin* remained on the lakes until going to saltwater in 1916 to serve briefly for the Nova Scotia Steel and Coal Company prior to its sale later that same year to William Wotherspoon of New York City. Having entered U.S. registry and operating for the American Star Line, this ship departed New York City for Britain on February 20, 1917 with a general cargo. Nearly three weeks later, on the morning of March 12, the *Algonquin* became the first U.S. flagged ship sunk to have left port after Germany declared its policy to begin unrestricted submarine warfare on February 1, 1917. Torpedoed by the German submarine *U-62* at a position 65 miles west of Bishops Rock off Cornwall, England, all 27 crewmen aboard the stricken vessel survived the sinking. As such, this ship was just one of several U.S. flagged ships lost to hostile action prior to the United States entering World War I on April 6, 1917.[23]

The last ship to report sighting the *Bannockburn*, the steamer *Huronic*, became a member of the Canada Steamship Lines following that firm's formation in 1913. Later restricted to hauling freight only, this vessel served in that fleet's Northern Navigation Division and remained active until December of 1949 when it tied up for the final time at Hamilton, Ontario. Scrapped at that port the following year, the *Huronic* suffered a number of accidents over its forty-seven year operational career. These include at least two separate groundings on Lake Superior and a major collision with the freighter *Dow*

Chemical (2) on Lake Huron in May of 1944.[24]

Launched in 1896, the *Frank Rockefeller* was one of 43 whaleback vessels built under the direction of Captain Alexander McDougall between 1887 and 1898. Three years after coming across flotsam likely to be from the sunken *Bannockburn*, this steamship suffered considerable damage when it ran onto the rocks on Isle Royale during an autumn gale in November 1905. Salvaged, the *Rockefeller* continued operating for the Pittsburgh Steamship Company until its 1927 sale to the Central Dredging Company. Renamed *South Park* and entering the stone and gravel trade, this ship passed through a number of owners before ending up in the Erie Steamship Company in 1936. Employed to haul grain and automobiles, this steamer then passed into the Nicholson-Universal Steamship Company fleet before its subsequent purchase by Cleveland Tankers in 1943. Converted into a tanker and renamed *Meteor*, this ship operated in the liquid bulk trade until suffering a grounding accident at Marquette, Michigan in 1969. Retired, the *Meteor* sat idle at Manitowoc, Wisconsin until 1972 when the city of Superior, Wisconsin acquired it for display as a museum ship. Its black hull showing the scars of a long and active operational career, this unique vessel remains in existence to this day not far from the place of its original construction.[25]

Without substantiating evidence, all of the theories surrounding this maritime disappearance remain nothing more than pure conjecture. It is, however, beyond question that the failure of the *Bannockburn* to make port in November of 1902 resulted in one of the most enduring mysteries in the annals of shipping on the Great Lakes. With over a century having passed since this disaster, the reasons behind the loss of this steamship remain as elusive as its final resting spot in the depths of Lake Superior.

Chapter Four
Lake Superior Claims Two More

History records that at just ten minutes before 1 o'clock in the afternoon of April 14, 1905, the 440-foot long steamer *Captain Thomas Wilson* made that season's first commercial passage through the Soo Locks at Sault Ste. Marie, Michigan. With the lock facility planning to commemorate its fiftieth anniversary with a semi-centennial celebration scheduled for August of that year, the beginning of shipping season picked up at a brisk pace with officials proudly anticipating up to 20 additional vessels to transit the canal that day. One such vessel was the steamer *Martin Mullen*, which arrived at Sault Ste. Marie just one hour after the *Wilson* made its upbound passage. Owned by the Lakewood Steamship Company as one of the several ships operating under the management of the Hutchinson & Company of Cleveland, Ohio, the *Mullen* was to play a minor role in the mystery surrounding the sinking of a wooden steamer and its consort barge on Lake Superior later that year.[1]

With every major sector of raw material transportation experiencing a significant increase in comparison to cargo movements from the preceding year, the 1905 shipping season was to prove a banner year for commerce on the Great Lakes. As the most heavily carried commodity, the iron ore trade was to peak at 33,476,904 gross tons, an increase of nearly 58-perecent over that shipped from lake ports during the previous season. With shipments of coal and grain also making substantial gains, shippers struggled to meet the boosted demand as their vessels plodded between various harbors on the lakes. Among the many U.S. flagged ships engaged in the movement of iron ore and grain that season was the steamer *Iosco* and its consort schooner-barge *Olive-Jeanette.*

Built in 1891 by the F. W. Wheeler & Company at West Bay City, Michigan, the *Iosco* was one of six nearly identical wooden steamers built by that yard over a three-year period stretching between 1890 and 1893. The other members of this class included the *C. F. Bielman, L. R. Doty, William F. Sauber, Tampa,* and *Uganda.* Remarkably, all of these steamers were to carry their original names throughout their entire operational careers. Proving to be a somewhat unlucky class, five of these vessels were destined to sink below the waters of the Great Lakes, including one intentionally scuttled after reaching the end of its useful life.

Named for a Michigan county located on the western shore of Lake Huron and bordering the northern reaches of Saginaw Bay, the *Iosco* entered service for the Hawgood & Avery Transit Company in early 1891. Measuring 312 feet in length, 41 feet in beam, and 20 feet in depth, the 2,051 gross-ton wooden steamer went to work in the iron ore and grain trades. For the next fourteen years, the *Iosco* operated without suffering any serious accidents with the exception of the usual minor episodes affecting lake freighters of that era during their regular voyages through hazardous navigation channels and sudden bouts with heavy weather. This steamer did make the news on one occasion; however, when on May 18, 1894 it became the first vessel to sail from Duluth after heavy seas led to a 48-hour delay in departures from that port with a two-foot rise in the harbor's water level, the latter of which also shut down two local sawmills.[2]

Just one year before the *Iosco* entered service, the F. W. Wheeler & Company had built another vessel for the Hawgood & Avery Transit Company in the form of the four-masted schooner *Olive-Jeanette*. Named for two daughters of Roger M. Munger, the president of the Imperial Mill Company, and possessing the impressive dimensions of a 249-foot length, 39-foot beam, and 16-foot depth, this vessel was one of the largest such ships ever constructed for service on the Great Lakes. Built primarily to move grain, the *Olive-Jeanette*, like many other schooners of the day, operated not as a sailing vessel but as a consort barge to maximize the tonnage carried on the towing steamer's revenue generating voyages. It was during one such trip in its first decade of service that this schooner-barge was nearly lost.[3]

Loaded with a cargo of corn, the *Olive-Jeanette* departed South Chicago, Illinois in tow of the steamer *L. R. Doty* on the night of October 24, 1898. Bound for the port of Midland, Ontario on Georgian Bay, the two vessels sailed northbound on Lake Michigan toward the Straits of Mackinac. Having proceeded several miles north of Milwaukee by the following evening, the towline connecting the schooner-barge to the *L. R. Doty* snapped during a fierce storm. Within moments, those aboard the

Seven years before its 1905 loss, the schooner *Olive-Jeanette* survived a storm that sank its towing steamer, *L. R. Doty*, in Lake Michigan.

Olive-Jeanette lost sight of their companion in the storm-tossed seas. As such, they were likely the last to see the *L. R. Doty* as that steamer disappeared into the depths of the lake a short time later along with it entire crew of seventeen.[4]

Aboard the *Olive-Jeanette*, Captain David Cadette used all his experience to keep his ship afloat even as Lake Michigan continued its relentless assault upon the wooden schooner. Cast adrift, the desperate crew scrambled to hoist sail as their vessel pitched and rolled in the turbulent waters. In addition to suffering some flooding of its cargo hold, the *Olive-Jeanette* also sustained a broken rudder and torn sails during a struggle for survival that stretched into three days.

On the morning of October 27, the combination

passenger and package steamer *City of Louisville* sighted the *Olive-Jeanette* in mid-lake. An additional report from the package freighter *Susquehanna* told of a four-masted barge drifting off Kenosha, Wisconsin. Observing no distress signals and believing the schooner to be handling the seas well, the captain of the 326-foot long steamer made no effort to render aid. News of these sightings led to a handful of tugboats sailing into the lake in an attempt to locate and retrieve the wandering vessel.[5]

While searching for the *Olive-Jeanette*, the tug *Prodigy* of the Independent Towing Line came across a large wreckage field approximately 25 miles off Kenosha that likely originated from the now missing *L. R. Doty*. Having set out from Chicago at noon in company with the tug *Mosher*, Captain John Hennessey of the tug *T. T. Morford* first sighted the waterlogged schooner-barge at 4 o'clock that afternoon. Taken in tow of the two tugs, the battered vessel began its journey back to Chicago, where it arrived at 5 o'clock in the morning of October 28. Despite the crew having continuously worked its pumps for seventy-two hours without relief, a survey revealed the *Olive-Jeanette* had over 30 inches of water in its cargo hold.[6]

In the wake of the *L. R. Doty* disappearance, newspaper reports carried a story relating a connection between the *Olive-Jeanette* and the twin daughters of the sunken steamer's master, Captain Christopher Smith of Port Huron, Michigan. As previously mentioned, the schooner-barge took its name from the daughters of the president of the Imperial Mill Company. Shortly after its launching, one of the original owners, P. C. Smith of

Saginaw, Michigan, named his twin daughters after the vessel. When twin girls were born to Captain Smith in 1896, he also reportedly chose to use the *Olive-Jeanette* as the inspiration in naming his own daughters.[7]

Following repairs, the *Olive-Jeanette* resumed its consort barge duties in the Hawgood & Avery Transit Company fleet. It was in this role that the schooner and its towing steamer, *Iosco*, took on cargoes of iron ore at Duluth on the morning of Thursday, August 31, 1905. Sailing out of the harbor at noon, the pair ventured into Lake Superior to begin the first leg of the downbound voyage to a Lake Erie port.[8]

Commanded by Captain Nelson Gonyaw of Bay City, Michigan, and powered by a triple-expansion steam engine, the *Iosco* carried a crew of nineteen. Benefiting from staffing requirements much lower than that of its towing steamer, the *Olive-Jeanette* employed a crew of seven under the leadership of Captain McGreavy. With a thick towline connecting the two vessels, the crews of both ships toiled at their respective duties on what most probably believed was to be just another routine trip down the lakes.[9]

Complicating the bustle associated with a significant uptick in the demand for the movement of raw materials, a series of storms disrupted shipping operations across the Lake Superior region during the latter half of the 1905 navigation season. Even as the *Iosco* and *Olive-Jeanette* departed upon their ill-fated voyage, a very early fall storm was approaching the most northern reaches of the Great Lakes. Reacting to the onset of the violent weather system, the U.S. Weather Bureau issued storm warnings for Lake Superior one day after the two ships had set sail. Unleashing its fury, the northeast gale assaulted the lake for the next two days with heavy rains and winds exceeding 40 miles per hour. Surprising many mariners with its ferocity, the storm stirred up the cold waters so severely that heavy seas prevailed for two full days following its passage.[10]

As the storm raged during the early hours of Saturday, September 2, Captain W. P. Benham of the steamer *William A. Paine* spotted the *Iosco* and *Olive-Jeanette* off Stannard Rock. Appearing to be making fair progress in the heavy seas, the two wooden vessels displayed no signs of any distress. Another sighting during the daylight hours of that same day by Captain Massey aboard the bulk carrier *Martin Mullen* placed the *Iosco* and its consort at a position some 20 miles east of the Huron Islands. Although both ships were taking a pounding from the angry lake, Massey felt neither seemed to be in any danger.[11]

At some point following these observations, Captain Nelson Gonyaw apparently abandoned his eastward journey toward Sault Ste. Marie with a turn to the west as the next sighting of either of these vessels took place the next day, when the keeper of the Huron Island Light spotted the *Olive-Jeanette* about four miles north of his station. Seeing no evidence of any accompanying steamer and unaware of his unexpected visitor's identity, the lighthouse keeper kept the consort barge in sight from atop his rocky island outpost until it foundered at 4 o'clock that afternoon.[12]

With the outside world unaware of the schooner's

sinking, other clues pointing toward a major maritime disaster began coming to light. On the same day that the keeper of the Huron Island Light witnessed the final hours of the *Olive-Jeanette*, the passenger steamer *Juniata* came across a field of wreckage 10 miles east of the Portage Entry. The following day, a large amount of debris began washing ashore along a section of coastline stretching from the property of the Huron Mountain Club located 30 miles northwest of Marquette and westward over a distance of some 40 miles to the small community of L'Anse, Michigan on Keweenaw Bay. While the scattered wreckage included hatch covers, a small boat, and pieces of a ship's cabin, the most telling find was the recovery of a nameboard stenciled with the word "Olive," a clear indication that the unfolding tragedy involved the schooner-barge *Olive-Jeanette* and one confirmed by the subsequent discovery of one of the vessel's oars.[13]

Following a 20-mile row in a small boat, the keeper of the Huron Island Light arrived at Pequaming, Michigan on Tuesday, September 5, to report the sinking of a large schooner. That same day, the tug *D. L. Hebard* came across a large wreckage field near the Huron Islands that contained a number of life preservers bearing the name "*Iosco*." In addition, the crew of the tug also found a body floating 10 miles off Point Abbaye. The discovery of the life preservers and the eyewitness account of the lighthouse keeper confirmed the loss of the steamer *Iosco* and its consort barge *Olive-Jeanette*.[14]

Concurrent with these developments, searchers began recovering bodies that came ashore between Keweenaw

Bay and the Huron Mountain Club. Wearing life preservers marked with the name of the missing steamer, the victims provided evidence suggesting the *Iosco*, like its consort-barge, foundered slowly with its crew having ample time to don life saving gear. With no survivors from either vessel, the double sinking resulted in the loss of twenty-six lives. In financial terms, the *Iosco* had an insurance value of $65,000 while the *Olive-Jeanette* represented a $40,000 loss.[15]

Even as Lake Superior yielded the first bits of wreckage from the *Iosco*, company officials back at the Hawgood Fleet's headquarters in Cleveland had already resigned themselves to the fact that their organization had lost two of its vessels. Speaking from his corporate office on September 7, William A. Hawgood, managing owner of the fleet, told marine reporters that his company had given up all hope of finding the *Iosco* and *Olive-Jeanette* or their crews. To assist in the recovery effort, the company

The steamer *Iosco* was one of six nearly identical wooden steamers constructed by the F. W. Wheeler & Company at West Bay City, Michigan during the early years of the 1890s.

dispatched Captain Smith to serve as its representative at Marquette.[16]

By September 12, recovery crews had located fifteen bodies from the two sunken vessels, among which included the remains of one woman believed to have been the wife of the *Iosco*'s cook who hailed from Fairport, Ohio. With a large portion of wreckage and victims coming ashore on and near the property owned by the Huron Mountain Club, the members of that organization assumed a prominent role in the search operation. This contribution included a small gasoline powered boat belonging to one of the members that began a series of regular shoreline patrols in the days immediately following the sinking. Reporting on the club's commitment to continue its quest for further victims indefinitely, that day's edition of Sault Ste. Marie, Michigan's *The Evening News* also related Captain Smith's realistic approach to the recovery operation with his statement, "it is probable that some of the bodies will never be found."[17]

Upon arriving at Marquette, the recovered bodies underwent an examination at the Hager Morgue. With at least one set of remains exhibiting a badly crushed skull, Coroner Crary recorded all of the pertinent information concerning the physical characteristics of each corpse to assist relatives in the identification process. After the coroner had finished his task, several of the bodies went into temporary storage in the receiving vault at that city's Park Cemetery. It would be at that location that officials later chose to inter five unidentified victims.[18]

To facilitate the recovery effort, managers at the

Hawgood & Co. employed the assistance of a local homesteader living near the Huron Mountain Club named J. J. Behrendt. Scouring the shore on foot and by boat on the evening of September 9, he came across the body of one sailor floating amongst an assortment of logs in a cove near an area known as the "Flat Rocks" some eight miles north of the clubhouse. While working his way toward the Huron Mountain Club the following afternoon, Behrendt discovered another victim five miles further down the coast near Huron River Point.[19]

With a search area extending between Granite Point and the Big Huron River, the team led by the homesteader covered a twenty-five mile long stretch of coastline. During one of its patrols, this group opened a macabre chapter in the loss of the *Iosco* and *Olive-Jeanette* by uncovering evidence of someone having pulled a body from the water at a point ten miles from the Huron Mountain Club. Along with a number of human footprints and drag marks across the ground, Behrendt also reported finding a strap from a pair of men's underwear bearing the initials "H. G." hanging from a nearby bush that apparently became detached when an unknown party pulled the body through the brush and toward the tree line. Although the initials printed on the recovered piece of fabric did not match those of Captain Nelson Gonyaw, many believed the body may have been that of *Iosco*'s skipper and that the letters could have instead been a laundry mark. Known to have carried about $800 on his person, the presence of a considerable amount of cash may have enticed someone to conceal the captain's body in an unmarked grave after deciding to

49

keep the money for themselves.[20]

In the end, the search effort resulted in the recovery of fifteen bodies from the double sinking, including eight found by members of the Huron Mountain Club. Despite his brother having traveled from lower Michigan to participate in the hunt for clues, the body of Captain Gonyaw, or its possible secret burial location, was never found. With the lake reluctant to give up any more of its dead, it was not until June of the following year that the final victim attributed to the two lost vessels was located near L'Anse.[21]

The eyewitness account provided by the keeper of the Huron Island Light concerning his observations on Sunday, September 3, leaves little doubt that the *Iosco* and *Olive-Jeanette* abandoned their eastward voyage at some point after the steamers *William A. Paine* and *Martin Mullen* sighted them in mid-lake the previous day. Struggling against the tempest, Captain Gonyaw likely decided to seek shelter behind one of the islands east of the Keweenaw Peninsula or possibly in the Keweenaw Waterway. The appearance of the *Olive-Jeanette* without the *Iosco* in the hours before it sank suggests the steamer foundered first, thus leaving its consort barge at the mercy of the weather.[22]

Other than the *Iosco* and *Olive-Jeanette*, the storm also led to the loss of two other vessels on Lake Superior. In the western section of the lake, the 390-foot long bulk carrier *Sevona* went hard aground on Sand Island Reef in the Apostle Islands just after 5 o'clock in the morning of September 2. Pounded by the heavy seas in its vulnerable position, the fifteen-year old steamer soon went to pieces with the loss of seven lives. Thirty miles northeast of Outer Island, the schooner-barge *Pretoria* suffered a broken rudder while in tow of the steamer *Venezuela*. After its towline parted, the five-year old wooden vessel quickly proved no match for the storm by sinking a short time later in 52 feet of water. Although the entire crew of ten managed to abandon the sinking vessel, half of them drowned when the lifeboat capsized in the turbulent waters.[23]

Elsewhere on Lake Superior, a large wave washed a watchman to his death from aboard the whaleback *Samuel Mather* (2) off Knife Island. Sixty miles east of Keweenaw Point, another man lost his life when heavy wave action carried away the second engineer of the Gilchrist steamer *R. L. Ireland*. The sailors aboard the steamer *Simon Langell* and its consort barges *Arenac, Interlaken,* and *W. K. Moore* proved far more fortunate when they arrived at Duluth on September 6 following a sixty-six hour battle with the lake. Heavily laden with cargoes of limestone, the four vessels survived their ordeal despite the wooden steamer suffering a broken steering cable that at one point left the vessels helpless in the waves for two long hours.[24]

Sailing into Duluth on September 6, Captain Charles Hahn of the steamer *Frank W. Gilchrist* wasted no time in criticizing the lack of storm signals at various points along his vessel's upbound journey from southern Lake Michigan to the head of the lakes. By doing so, he attested to the suddenness and unexpected ferocity of the early fall storm. With his own vessel initially believed to be among those lost in the gale, Hahn told marine reporters, "From the time we left Chicago until we reached Sault Ste. Marie we did not see a single storm signal to give us warning. I looked carefully for some warning at Sheboygan, Mackinac, and other points, but to no purpose."[25]

Found sitting upright, the badly mangled wreck of the *Olive-Jeanette* lies off Huron Island in 290 feet of water. In the darkness at that depth, the preserving qualities of the lake have allowed the faded letters of the schooner's name to remain visible in spite of spending over a century underwater. By continuing to elude the efforts of human exploration, however, the final resting spot of the steamer *Iosco* remains an enigma in the history of Lake Superior shipwrecks.

Chapter Five
Vanished From Sight

During the early afternoon hours of April 26, 1890 a feeling of excitement reverberated throughout the community of Kingston, Ontario. Located at the eastern end of Lake Ontario, the city's waterfront was to play host to a crowd numbering in the thousands that had gathered to witness the launch of the schooner *Minnedosa*. Built by the Montreal Transportation Company, the design of the four-masted sailing vessel incorporated a respectable 250-foot length, 36-foot 3-inch beam, and a 15-foot 1 inch depth. Although smaller in size to the U.S. flagged five-masted schooner *David Dows* lost just six months earlier in a storm on Lake Michigan, the *Minnedosa* was to be the largest such vessel ever built in Canada for service on the Great Lakes.

The scheduled launch that afternoon soon went awry, however, when the schooner refused to slide into the water. With the *Minnedosa* remaining stubbornly stationary, a diver descended below the launch ways the following afternoon to remove a wooden timber believed to be holding the vessel up. This delicate operation having proven successful, the shipyard decided to make another launch attempt at 7 o'clock that evening. About a half hour later, a crowd numbering around 4,000 emitted a deafening cheer as the schooner began moving slowly down the launching ways. Picking up speed as it covered the last few feet to the water's edge, the *Minnedosa* entered its natural element a few moments later with a large splash.[1]

Fitted with anchors and chain while secured at a wharf at the foot of Queen Street on the morning of Monday, April 28, the schooner had its rudder adjusted a few hours later after a tug moved it into deeper water. Towed by the tug *Thompson*, the *Minnedosa* began its maiden voyage later that evening when it departed Kingston bound to load a return cargo of grain at Duluth, Minnesota.[2]

Despite its impressive size, the construction of the *Minnedosa* came during the waning days of commercial sailing vessels on the Great Lakes. As part of this transition, several schooners found second careers as barges towed on their voyages by tugboats or steam-powered freighters. This trend extended to include even the largest and newest sailing vessels built in shipyards around the lakes. For example, the before mentioned *David Dows* spent the majority of its short eight-year career as a barge. Although fully rigged as a schooner, the *Minnedosa* was destined to serve its entire operational career as a schooner-barge towed by a tug or one of the company's steamers.[3]

Commonly termed as consort barges, the employment of these craft allowed ship operators to transport significantly more cargo on each trip at the cost of a slight reduction in speed and an equally negligible increase in crew size. Although the construction of larger steel freighters during the first quarter of the twentieth century was to render this practice obsolete, the concept remained in use, on a small scale, well into the early 1960s.[4]

Placing its new schooner into service as one of the forty-one vessels built in Ontario for the Canadian fleet in 1890, the Montreal Transportation Company frequently paired the *Minnedosa* with the ill-fated steamer *Bannockburn* during its early career. Engaged in the grain trade, the schooner operated primarily between grain loading ports on Lake Superior and Kingston.[5]

On the morning of October 18, 1905, the fifteen-year-old *Minnedosa* sat below the loading spouts at Fort William, Ontario as a stream of wheat flowed into its cargo hold. Nearby, two fleet mates, the steel steamer *Westmount* (1) and the schooner *Melrose,* were also taking aboard grain cargoes in preparation to make an early fall voyage to Kingston. With the last of the 75,000-bushel wheat payload aboard, the crew went to work securing the schooner's hatches as Captain John Phillips prepared his vessel for departure.

Hailing from Kingston, Captain Phillips had gained experience commanding two other barges belonging to the company's fleet. This included a three-year stint aboard the *Dunmore* during a period stretching from 1899 and 1901 followed by serving as captain of the barge *Quebec* during the 1902 and 1903 seasons. The balance of the schooner's small crew consisted of First Mate Arthur Waller and James Allen, both of Nova Scotia, George McDermott of Belleview, Ontario, and three unidentified sailors believed to have come from the Kingston area. Also aboard the *Minnedosa* on this particular voyage was the wife of Captain Phillips and an unnamed passenger.[6]

With all three vessels loaded for the downbound trip, the *Westmount* (1) took up the slack in the steel cable connecting its stern to the bow of the *Minnedosa*, which was itself attached to the schooner *Melrose* by a heavy hawser. As smoke billowed heavily from its stack, the steamer began the 1,000-mile voyage by pulling the two barges into an angry Lake Superior already stirred up by a brisk autumn wind.

Following a choppy, but ultimately uneventful, trip across the wide expanse of Lake Superior, the trio passed through the locks at Sault Ste. Marie the next morning. Proceeding down the lower section of the St. Marys River

Although constructed with four masts, the large wooden schooner *Minnedosa* spent its entire career as a schooner-barge.

throughout the balance of the day, the trio passed De Tour, Michigan just as darkness fell. Leaving the small community in their wake, the three vessels ventured into upper Lake Huron in the face of a stiffening northeast wind. Growing quickly in intensity, the worsening conditions brought winds in excess of 40 miles per hour along with heavy snow and freezing spray.

Aboard the *Westmount* (1), Captain Alexander Milligan considered the rapidly deteriorating weather as he plotted a southbound course toward Port Huron. After wallowing in heavy seas for a few hours, a shift in the wind to the northwest provided the steamer and its two companions the opportunity to seek the lee offered by the Michigan shore. With his two-year old vessel exhibiting no signs of undue stress given the prevailing conditions, Milligan's primary concern centered upon the welfare of the two heavily laden schooners. Other than the towline attached to *Minnedosa* still showing tension, the only evidence of the two schooner-barges still being astern of the steamer was an occasional sighting of their bobbing lights through breaks in the snow.

Hugging the coastline until reaching the vicinity of Oscoda, Captain Milligan turned the *Westmount* (1) southeast to begin the 40-mile run across Saginaw Bay toward the tip of Michigan's "thumb." Although necessary to continue the downbound voyage, this course change took the three vessels out of the calmer inshore waters and exposed them to the full power of the storm. Facing the onslaught, the crews of the *Minnedosa* and *Melrose* struggled to keep their ships from taking on water as the hulls of the old wooden vessels strained against a ceaseless procession of waves stirred up by the open waters of the bay.

Successfully completing their trek across Saginaw Bay, the three vessels once more took advantage of the protection offered by the lee of the Michigan shore. By this time, however, the damage had been done. The mauling suffered by the *Minnedosa* and *Melrose* over the past few hours had left both vessels in very poor shape. Standing in the pilothouse of the *Westmount* (1), there could have been little doubt in the mind of Captain Milligan that the two consorts had taken a severe beating despite neither displaying any distress signals.

As the trio neared Harbor Beach during the final minutes of October 20, 1905, the *Minnedosa* suddenly vanished into the depths of Lake Huron. Just moments before its companion plunged to the bottom, the crew of the *Melrose* felt a sudden snap as the towline connecting their vessel to the lost schooner parted. Pulling the hawser aboard, the crew quickly discovered the line bore the unmistakable scars of being cut through by an axe rather than breaking from the stresses placed upon it by the storm. Set helplessly adrift, the strong winds began pushing the *Melrose* toward the middle of the lake.[7]

Shortly after the *Minnedosa* disappeared from sight, Captain Milligan took the *Westmount* (1) through a perilous 180-degree turn to begin a search for the two consort barges. At the stern of the bulk carrier, the crew busied itself to recover the now useless steel towline. Pulling the last of the line from the water, they discovered the tow post of the *Minnedosa* still attached to the end of the heavy cable. Rolling heavily in rough seas and fighting its way out of the trough of the waves, the steel steamer began retracing its course northbound. Despite its best efforts, the crew of the *Westmount* (1) found no trace of the nine persons aboard the schooner at the time of its loss.[8]

Unable to assist those lost aboard the *Minnedosa*, Captain Milligan turned his attention toward retrieving the *Melrose* to prevent an even larger loss of life. In the hours ahead, the *Westmount* (1) made several failed attempts to attach a line to the drifting schooner before finally succeeding just before 5 o'clock that morning some 20 miles offshore. Finding the *Melrose* precariously close to sinking, Milligan set course for the safety of Harbor Beach, where the pair arrived later that afternoon.[9]

Recounting the events of that day, Captain R. H. Davey told of his crew and passengers never expecting to see land again while drifting helplessly in the maelstrom. Among those aboard were the captain's wife, daughter, and young son. Ignoring the panicked pleas of his wife and daughter to remain in the cabin, Davey rushed between the cabin and the deck as he did everything humanly possible to keep the *Melrose* afloat. With a flooded cabin and shattered bulkwarks, the schooner barely survived the heavy seas while awaiting the *Westmount* (1) to secure a towing hawser.[10]

Commenting upon the loss of the *Minnedosa*, Captain Milligan described the 75,000 bushels of wheat carried aboard the schooner on its final voyage to news reporters as being 15,000 bushels in excess of its normal payload. Although expressing his opinion that such a cargo was perfectly safe for the schooner to carry, Milligan also implied the economic pressures that may influenced Captain Phillips' decision to load a heavier than normal payload with the statement, "It was too late in the season and rates were high."[11]

The same storm system that led to the demise of the *Minnedosa* caused widespread damage across the Great Lakes region. On Lake Michigan, the schooner *John V. Jones* capsized close to the Wisconsin shore with the loss of two lives. Amazingly, a salvage operation allowed the twenty-nine year old vessel to sail for another nine seasons until its owners abandoned the aged schooner in 1914.[12]

In northern Lake Huron, the tug *Frank Perry* foundered near Port Dolomite. Further south, heavy seas forced the steamer *Joseph S. Fay* ashore near Rogers City while also stranding its consort barge *D. P. Rhodes* near Cheboygan. Although storm action soon battered the helpless steamer to pieces, the *Rhodes* survived until its sale for scrapping in 1938 following several years of service in a non-transportation role on the lower St. Lawrence River. South of the *Joseph S. Fay* stranding, the schooner *Emma L. Nielson* suffered severe damage after grounding in Presque Isle Harbor. Refloated, the schooner sailed until 1911 when it went to the bottom of Lake Huron following a collision with the steamer *Wyandotte* (3) off East Tawas, Michigan.[13]

Although not reported as missing until four days after the storm, the most serious loss on Lake Huron proved to be the disappearance of the wooden steamer *Kaliyuga* with seventeen lives. With Captain Fred L. Tonkin in command and locking downbound at the Soo Locks on the same day as the *Minnedosa* and its two companions, the 280-foot steamer had loaded a cargo of iron ore destined for Cleveland before departing Marquette on its final voyage. Believed to have foundered in northern Lake Huron, the wreck of the *Kaliyuga* remains elusive to this day.[14]

Continuing its eastward march, the storm continued its path of destruction on Lake Erie. The most significant loss in terms of lives lost on the lake was the sinking of the schooner *Tasmania* approximately 2½ miles southwest of the Southeast Shoal lightship. In tow of the steamer *Bulgaria* at the time of its loss, the 34-year old schooner carried its entire crew of eight men to their deaths. To the east, the Gilchrist steamer *Siberia* went ashore off Long Point. Its entire crew rescued by the steamer *J. H. Wade*, the stranded bulk carrier became a total loss when it broke up a few days later.[15]

On the south shore of the lake, the tug *Walter Metcalf* sank at Cleveland while heavy wave action pushed the steamer *Sarah E. Sheldon* ashore near Lorain, Ohio. In that vulnerable position not far from the site of its original construction 33 years earlier, continued storm action broke up the wooden bulk freighter later that day. Losing its battle with the storm, the schooner *Mautenee* stranded near Ripley, New York. Abandoned in place by its owners, the wooden sailing vessel went to pieces over the following two months. Other losses on Lake Erie included the schooners *Commerce* and *Yukon*, the latter of which sank off Ashtabula, Ohio.[16]

Within days of its loss, a sensational report began appearing in newspapers across the nation that told of the *Minnedosa*'s crew heroically cutting the heavy hawser attaching their vessel to the lumbering *Melrose*. Originating from Port Huron, Michigan and incorporating elements no living person had witnessed, this report described the disaster with phrases such as, "The angered, raging wind sent mountainous waves to batter to pieces the wooden boat," and "Captain Jack Phillips' voice rose in command over the howling storm." Consequently, this popular narrative read more like a folk tale rather than a fact-based account. While such stories make for interesting reading, it obscures the possibility that Captain Phillips may have ordered the line cut in a desperate effort to save his own vessel.[17]

With temporary repairs completed, the *Westmount* (1) and *Melrose* departed Harbor Beach for Kingston. After sailing 60 miles south, the pair reached Sarnia, Ontario to enter the St. Clair River before continuing through the connecting channels to Lake Erie. Crossing that body of water without incident and with the *Melrose* still showing signs of its battle on Lake Huron, the two vessels passed through the Welland Canal and across Lake Ontario to arrive at Kingston on October 26, 1905.[18]

By this time, and possibly after conferring with fleet managers, Captain Milligan had retracted his earlier published statements concerning the possible overloaded condition of the *Minnedosa* on its final voyage. In addition, he also stated his view, "that the vessel *Minnedosa* took in, through leaking, water enough to cause her to suddenly settle." Speaking to the media at Ottawa, Ontario, the following day, C. F. Gildersleeve, president of the Dominion Marine Insurance Company, supported Milligan's amended position by also expressing the opinion that the schooner foundered from leaking rather than overloading. During this session, the insurance executive also said his company would not object to any regulatory actions to prevent the overloading of vessels.[19]

Unlike most of the ships that have sailed into oblivion on the waters of the Great Lakes, the disappearance of the *Minnedosa* took place within sight of two other vessels. As such, there was little mystery as to the events leading up to the schooner's sudden plunge to the bottom of the lake. Considering the beating the *Minnedosa* had taken in its heavily laden condition, it is almost certain that the rough seas forced open the old wooden vessel's seams. With water flooding into its hull, the schooner progressively settled deeper into the lake until it reached a point at which its foundering was an unavoidable conclusion to the ill-fated voyage.

Although no doubt exists as to someone intentionally cutting the line attaching the *Minnedosa* to the *Melrose*, it is impossible to ascertain the exact circumstances leading up to this act. Is it possible that Captain Phillips, in a moment of desperation, ordered the hawser severed to reduce the strain on his own foundering vessel? On the other hand, could it have truly been a final compassionate act on behalf of the doomed crew to prevent their vessel from also dragging the *Melrose* down? Whatever the true motive, those aboard the *Minnedosa* took the answer to this mystery to their watery graves.

Following the loss of the *Minnedosa*, the *Westmount* (1) continued to operate in the grain trade until its sale to

Inter-American Steamship Company, Ltd. of Toronto, Ontario in 1915. Entering service on salt water under the name *Wethersfield*, this vessel passed through a series of owners before its sale into German registry and renaming to *Max Bernstein* in 1923. Converted into an automobile and tractor carrier in 1926, this ship operated under the name *Fordson I* and later as the *Tractor*. It was under the latter name that this vessel returned briefly to the Great Lakes during the 1928 and 1932 seasons. Renamed *Ludolf Oldendorff* in 1937, this vessel lasted until British aircraft sank it at Egersund, Norway on October 9, 1944.[20]

Although generally believed to have been only a few miles off Harbor Beach at the time of its sinking, the final resting spot of the lost schooner remained an enigma until its discovery several miles away from that location in May of 1993. Found at the culmination of a fifteen-year search encompassing some 700 square miles of the lake bottom, the wreck of the *Minnedosa* lies on an even keel in 210 feet of water 16 miles north of Harbor Beach. While exploring the sunken vessel a short time later, divers found the cleanly cut towing rope that once connected the schooner to the *Melrose* remarkably well preserved despite lying underwater for nearly ninety years.[21]

Chapter Six
Destined for Disaster

Even as the steamer *Iosco* and its consort-barge *Olive-Jeanette* labored in the fierce gale raging across the Lake Superior region on September 2, 1905, the crew of the steel bulk carrier *D. M. Clemson* was involved in its own struggle for survival in the western part of the lake. Despite being only two years old at the time and considered to be one of the staunchest vessels on the Great Lakes, the *Clemson* soon came out second best in its contest with the power of nature when heavy seas carried away two of its wooden hatch covers. With tons of water flooding into its cargo hold as the waves continued a relentless assault, the steamer began settling lower in the water. The safety of his ship and crew now placed in extreme jeopardy, Captain Samuel R. Chamberlain had little choice but to abandon his downbound voyage and seek shelter from the weather. After battling the storm for several hours, the *D. M. Clemson* limped slowly into Two Harbors, Minnesota, a major iron ore shipping port located 25 miles north of Duluth. Once inside the safety of the harbor's breakwaters, the crew took stock of the damage sustained in the storm. Having lost some of its railings and with flooding causing a four-foot list to starboard, the steamer was fortunate to have reached port. The near brush with disaster quickly forgotten, the completion of repairs soon had the *Clemson* back to work transporting raw materials across the lakes.[1]

In 1890, the longest ship in service on the Great Lakes measured 350 feet in length. Through a steady march of progress, that decade witnessed the largest vessels on the lakes grow to just over 400 feet long just five short years later. With this trend continuing into the early years of the twentieth century, lake steamers approached the 500-foot mark with the launching of the 497-foot long *John W. Gates* at Lorain, Ohio on January 20, 1900.

As ship owners struggled to meet a growing demand to move raw materials across the Great Lakes that was to more than double between 1900 and 1907, the early twentieth century saw a flurry of activity as shipbuilders turned out increasingly larger vessels. Among the many lake freighters to make their maiden voyages during this period was the steel bulk carrier *D. M. Clemson*. Built by the Superior Shipbuilding Company at West Superior, Wisconsin for Augustus B. Wolvin's Provident Steamship Company, the launching of this vessel took place on May 20, 1903. Powered by a 1,800 indicated horsepower quadruple-expansion engine and measuring 468 feet in length, 52 feet in beam, and 28 in depth, this steamer had a 7,800-ton carrying capacity. These design characteristics placed the *D. M. Clemson* among the largest freighters operating on the Great Lakes when it entered service in June of that year.[2]

Put to work moving iron ore from the upper reaches of the Great Lakes to receiving ports on the lower lakes, the *D. M. Clemson* often carried upbound cargoes of coal to avoid costly trips in ballast. It was on one such voyage when this vessel went aground at Bar Point near the mouth of the Detroit River on April 13, 1906. Released with the assistance of a tugboat a short time later, the steamer apparently suffered no serious harm in the incident. A more serious occurrence took place a little more than one year later when, on June 20, 1907, the *D. M. Clemson* collided with the whaleback steamer *James B. Neilson* off Middle Island in Lake Huron. Taking place in heavy fog, the *Clemson* suffered considerable damage in its unfortunate encounter with the Pittsburgh Steamship Company vessel.[3]

The latter months of the 1908 navigation season was to see the *D. M. Clemson* involved in a series of incidents, the last of which was to result in its loss. While attempting to enter Ashtabula in heavy seas on October 20 of that year, this steamer suffered several broken hull plates when the difficult conditions forced it into the inner side of the harbor's breakwater. Suffering some flooding through a puncture at the water line, the *Clemson* required temporary repairs before departing on its next voyage. Its string of bad luck on Lake Erie continuing, this vessel stranded on Point Pelee just four days later. Forced aground in stormy conditions, the steamer managed to free itself a short time later with no apparent damage.[4]

With his vessel having spent Thanksgiving Day idle just two days earlier, it is likely that Captain Samuel R. Chamberlain was anxious to get underway when the *D. M. Clemson* cleared Lorain, Ohio on November 28, 1908 with a load of coal destined for delivery to Superior, Wisconsin. Scheduled to enter winter layup after unloading this cargo, this was to be the ship's final trip of the season. Proceeding across Lake Erie and up the Detroit River before transiting Lake St. Clair and the St. Clair River, the bulk carrier entered Lake Huron. Carrying a crew of twenty-four, the *Clemson* worked its way up the St. Marys River to Sault Ste. Marie, Ontario. There, it made an uneventful passage through the Canadian lock at 9:30 in the morning of November 30. Among the vessels making upbound transits around the same time that cold autumn morning was the 452-foot long steamer *J. J. H. Brown*.[5]

Owned by the Brown Steamship Company and barely six months into its operational career, the *J. J. H. Brown* had entered service on May 14 of that year when it departed Buffalo, New York with a cargo of coal for Duluth. With Captain Frank B. Chamberlain as its master, this particular voyage was to take the steamer on another visit to the Minnesota port, where it would load a late season grain cargo destined for a lower lakes port. In company with the *D. M. Clemson*, the *J. J. H. Brown* picked up speed as both ships pulled away from the canal to begin sailing toward the more open waters of Whitefish Bay.[6]

Reaching the bay, the pair steamed northward an additional 25 miles before passing Whitefish Point. On the bridge of the *D. M. Clemson*, Captain Chamberlain had three possible courses to choose from in planning the route upon which his vessel would traverse the length of the frigid lake. Choosing the northern course would take his ship from Whitefish Point to the north of Michipicoten Island and along Superior's north shore and around Isle Royale before heading south into the Twin Ports.

Although the most lengthy and time consuming of the available routes, this course provided some protection from autumn storms that commonly plague the lake at that time of year. Unsurprisingly, the straight course involved sailing directly across the southern half of Lake Superior and around Manitou Island and the tip of the Keweenaw Peninsula before continuing toward Duluth. Generally similar to the straight course, the southern course followed the Michigan shore and involved a transit of the Keweenaw Waterway before continuing across the western section of the lake. Although shorter in distance, the southern and straight courses exposed vessels to the full brunt of northeast and northwest gales that could unleash their fury over distances reaching up to 150 miles of open water.[7]

Having decided to take his relatively new vessel across Lake Superior on the more prudent northern route, Captain Frank Chamberlain aboard the *J. J. H. Brown* watched as his counterpart on the *D. M. Clemson* turned west to pursue a southern course after passing Whitefish Point. With his vessel entering a heavy snow squall a short time later; however, the seasoned master of the *Brown* had little time to contemplate the wisdom of Samuel Chamberlain's decision to take the more exposed route. Sailing into whiteout conditions, he quickly lost sight of the *Clemson*. Continuing on course, the *J. J. H. Brown* ran into a heavy gale after sailing 75 miles up the lake. Later described by Captain Chamberlain as the worst he had ever seen, the gale pounded his vessel mercilessly as it struggled across the northern waters of Superior. Despite drifting for 12 hours with its engine shut down, the *J. J. H. Brown* proved itself a credit to its builders when it docked at Duluth one day behind schedule with minimal storm damage. Recounting the voyage aboard his nearly new vessel, Frank Chamberlain remarked, "It was the first test my boat ever got and I don't think she will ever get another like it. I know now what she can stand."[8]

The first indication that the gale had claimed a vessel came on December 4 when the crews of the steamer *Turret Court* and the package freighter *Wasaga* arrived at the Soo Locks with reports of passing through some wreckage off Crisp Point. With the debris field containing the top of a pilothouse and a collection of wood hatches, there was considerable concern that the flotsam might have come from the 310-foot long wooden steamer *Tampa* known to have been in that area when the storm struck. Covered with a layer of ice measuring up to 5 inches thick, the battered bulk carrier put all fears of its loss to rest when it arrived at Fort William, Ontario at 4 o'clock the following afternoon. A sister ship to the steamer *Iosco* lost on Lake Superior just three years earlier, the *Tampa* remained active until it sank in a collision during the 1911 shipping season. Subsequently raised from the bottom of the Detroit River in 1914, this vessel sat at Sarnia, Ontario prior to its scrapping the following year.[9]

The failure of the *D. M. Clemson* to make port in the days immediately following the storm prompted some concern for its welfare. As a survivor of many autumn storms, including a major blow just a few weeks earlier, few could imagine the modern steel freighter meeting an unfortunate end. As the hours passed without any sign of the *Clemson*, however, a feeling of dread began to kindle among those awaiting its arrival. Although word of an unknown ship sheltering behind Grand Island off Munising, Michigan provided a small glimmer of hope to fleet officials at Duluth, a subsequent report identified that vessel as actually being the wooden steamer *David W. Mills*.[10]

On December 6, six days after the *Clemson* had cleared Sault Ste. Marie, tugs began a search along the southern shore of Lake Superior for the overdue vessel. Venturing out into the cold waters, the crews embarked upon the tedious task of scouting behind every possible sheltering point and river mouth in the hope of finding some trace of the missing bulk carrier. The search effort expanded with each vessel transiting the lake keeping an extra watch for any sign of the *D. M. Clemson* or its crew while officials at the Soo Locks questioned every downbound vessel. In addition, a tug dispatched from Fort William scoured several miles of coastline only to reach Eagle Harbor without result.[11]

Although composed of individuals from across the Great Lakes region, many of the *Clemson*'s crew had made their homes in the Duluth area. As such, the dreadful news of the missing steamer spread quickly throughout the northern community. Of the ship's officers, Captain Samuel R. Chamberlain, First Mate W. A. McLeod, Second Mate Charles Woods, and Chief Engineer J. J. McCoy all came from that city. With anxious family members of the crew having besieged his offices for several days and after any hope of finding the vessel disabled had evaporated, Augustus B. Wolvin admitted to marine reporters on the evening of December 6, "The *Clemson* undoubtedly is at the bottom of the lake."[12]

Despite the foreboding statement by the vessel's owner, it had been impossible to attribute any of the early sightings of wreckage to the *D. M. Clemson*. Could this debris have instead come from the steel package freighter *Northern Queen* (2) of the Mutual Transit Company that was also overdue? With a temporary patch covering a large hole a few feet above the waterline caused by a collision in Lake Huron just one week earlier that resulted in the loss of its fleet mate *North Star* (1) and sailing the exposed southern course across Lake Superior, many began to wonder if the 312-foot steamer had survived the gale. Just as when all hope seemed lost, however, the *Northern Queen* (2) steamed into an ice-covered Portage Lake to reach Houghton, Michigan seemingly oblivious to the concern it had generated.[13]

In addition to being his steamer's last scheduled trip of the season, this particular voyage was also significant in that Captain Samuel Chamberlain planned to close out a thirty-year career on the lakes when the *D. M. Clemson* tied up at Superior. From the family home at Duluth, Mrs. Chamberlain refused to surrender any remaining hope of her husband's safe return by saying, "He is a skillful navigator, knows every nook and corner of the Great Lakes and if there is a possible method of escape, he can be depended upon."[14]

With the list of overdue ships becoming increasingly shorter, the continued absence of the *D. M. Clemson*

A survivor of the storm that sank the *Iosco* and *Olive-Jeanette*, the exact location at which the steamer *D. M. Clemson* lies on the bottom of Lake Superior remains a mystery.

assumed a more ominous character. In the midst of the early search, the steamer *George W. Peavey* arrived at Duluth with a report of the *Clemson* wrecked on the north shore of the lake with its entire crew safe. Although generating some renewed optimism, many doubted the veracity of this report. One person to provide such evidence was Captain Frank Chamberlain of the *J. J. H. Brown*. Although the last person known to have seen the ill-fated bulk carrier as it faded from sight in the snow just above Whitefish Point, Chamberlain did not learn of that vessel's disappearance until locking downbound at the Soo on December 7 on the return voyage from Duluth. Tying up his ship at the Kemp Coal Dock, he went to the nearby offices at the Soo Locks. There, Captain Chamberlain provided his account of the gale encountered the previous week. Describing the ferocity of the storm, he commented, "If the *Clemson* hasn't been heard from yet, she is on the bottom without a doubt." Disputing the accuracy of the report provided by the crew of the *Peavey*, the veteran shipmaster remarked, "I don't think she got to the north shore."[15]

Having departed Duluth with instructions from Augustus B. Wolvin to keep a sharp lookout for the *D. M. Clemson*, Captain Tilden of the missing vessel's fleet mate *James H. Hoyt* scouted the north shore and behind several islands during his voyage across the lake. Arriving at Sault Ste. Marie during the afternoon of December 7, the *Hoyt's* master also disputed rumors of the *Clemson* being ashore. Sending a series of telegrams to his company's office back at Duluth describing his downbound trip, Tilden reported finding no evidence of the lost freighter. Passing upbound at the locks later that evening, the steamers *Frank T. Heffelfinger* and *Frederick B. Wells* of Wolvin's Peavey Steamship Company also made a concerted effort to search for the *D. M. Clemson* during their westbound transits of Lake Superior.[16]

While the hunt for clues continued on the lake, debris began slowly making its way to shore. By December 8, searchers had recovered thirty wooden hatch covers from a 5-mile stretch of coastline extending from Vermillion Point west to Crisp Point. Painted red and measuring roughly 3x8 feet in size, the hatch covers came ashore along with the piece of a ship's cabin. Although clearly pointing a major shipping disaster, none of the recovered wreckage was immediately identifiable as belonging to the *D. M. Clemson*.[17]

Arriving at the Soo Locks on the night of December 8,

the captain of the *William H. Gratwick* reported passing through a debris field off Whitefish Point. Although the steamer did not sail close enough for its crew to make a detailed inspection of the flotsam, the prevailing opinion onboard was that some of the wreckage consisted of wooden hatch covers. That same day, a telegraph received at Detroit, Michigan from Port Arthur stated that Captain Zealand of the package freighter *Dundee* had positively identified some wreckage his vessel passed through as coming from the *D. M. Clemson*.[18]

At Buffalo when he first learned of the *Clemson's* disappearance, Will Chamberlain, son of the missing steamer's skipper, rushed northward to Duluth. After spending several days awaiting word at the ship owner's offices without result, he left for Grand Marais, Michigan to participate in the search. Wasting little time, the young Chamberlain began patrolling the beach between that village and Crisp Point in a quest to locate any debris or bodies from his father's ship. Joining him in this effort was Joseph S. Hayes, a company representative sent from the home office to organize a search party and assist in identifying any recovered wreckage. In the company of the fleet official and another companion from Duluth, Will Chamberlain continued to scout the shore above Whitefish Point until all three returned to that city near the middle of the month.[19]

Although there was no question as to the *D. M. Clemson* being the source of the various pieces of debris floating ashore on the beaches west of Whitefish Point, definitive proof of its loss came on December 10 with the recovery of a life preserver and a water barrel bearing the vessel's name near Crisp Point. The following day, the Peavey Steamship Company bulk carrier *Frederick B. Wells* arrived at Fort William with two hatch covers plucked from the water off Whitefish Point that were also identified as coming from the sunken steamer.[20]

As winter increased its grip on the upper lakes region with each passing day, officials had little choice but to scale back the number of beach patrols while tugboats began returning to port after abandoning their searches. Despite the abundance of wreckage gathered during the initial recovery operation, there was no sign of the *Clemson*'s lifeboats or the bodies of any of its crew. This suggested that whatever overcame the steamer happened very quickly with those aboard having little chance to abandon ship. Based upon the recovered wreckage, it was widely believed that the *D. M. Clemson* sank somewhere between Whitefish Point and Crisp Point in an area known to sailors of the day as the "Graveyard of the Lakes" for its abundance of shipwrecks.[21]

With the end of the shipping season looming on the horizon, traffic on Lake Superior became more sporadic as vessels rushed to make their final trips before the formation of heavy ice shut down the Soo Locks. Of the eleven ships reported as being at the twin ports of Port Arthur and Fort William on December 10 of that year, several planned to make one last grain run before the season ended. The expiration of insurance just a few days earlier meant such vessels not granted an extension would be traveling at their own risk during one of the most treacherous times of the year. While making their downbound voyages, a number of these ships reported seeing wreckage assumed to have originated from the *D. M. Clemson*.[22]

On the evening of December 14, 1908, the combination passenger and package steamer *Thomas Friant* arrived at Sault Ste. Marie as that season's last downbound ship from Lake Superior. During the voyage, Captain Joseph Rouleau and the crew of the small 101-foot long wooden vessel maintained a steady lookout for debris and bodies, an effort that ended without result.[23]

By this time, the families of those who perished in the sinking had resigned themselves to the unfortunate reality that it was unlikely that Lake Superior would surrender any of the dead crew. This changed on December 15, when the keeper of the Crisp Point Lighthouse spotted a body floating just offshore while he was in the process of closing the light for the winter. Although the keeper and his assistant attempted to retrieve the body by pulling it onto the ice extending from shore, it slipped from their grip and back into the cold lake waters. A subsequent search turned up nothing before the approach of nightfall curtailed any further recovery activities until the following day when an effort by life-saving crews from the Crisp Point and Two Heart River stations proved equally fruitless.[24]

Even as the life-savers scoured the shoreline, a rural postal carrier discovered a body four miles east of the Vermillion Life-Saving Station. Taken first to the station and then 30 miles south to Eckerman, Michigan, the victim arrived at Sault Ste. Marie by train shortly after 9 o'clock in the evening of December 18, 1908. Attesting to the frigid nature of Lake Superior in winter, Coroner A.

R. Haist found the body in an excellent state of preservation while performing an autopsy at a local morgue. Determined to be approximately 30 years in age and weighing between 200 and 225 pounds, the most identifiable feature on the man's body was a tattoo on his left forearm depicting a sailor and a maiden in an embrace. The only content of a pocketbook found on the remains proved to be a check good for 5 cents in trade at a Two Harbors pool hall.[25]

Although wearing a life preserver, the scantily clad body, which many believed to have been that of a fireman or oiler, suggested the *Clemson* sank quickly. The nature of the man's clothing implied he left his berth quickly with little time to escape the sinking vessel. During the few seconds available under such circumstances, he somehow managed to don a life preserver in a final desperate bid to increase his chances of survival.[26]

News of the unhappy discovery prompted a brother of Second Mate Charles Woods, to undertake a wintry 300-mile trek north from Marine City, Michigan to view the body. Serving as second engineer aboard the *William P. Palmer* (1) of the Pittsburgh Steamship fleet and with several brothers serving on other lake vessels, James Woods was well acquainted with the dangers of sailing the waters of the Great Lakes. Although finding it generally similar in height and weight, Woods claimed the body in the morgue had nothing else in common with his brother. With no family members coming forward to claim the body, officials enlisted the assistance of several persons connected to the city's waterfront, among which included one young boy engaged in selling newspapers along the canal. While many of these witnesses claimed to have recognized the man as coming from the ill-fated ship, none knew his name.[27]

Three days after the body arrived at Sault Ste. Marie, Reverend Thomas R. Easterday returned to that city after spending several days in the Whitefish Point area. He claimed that when first discovered, recovery personnel found a card in the victim's clothing that despite being without identification did indicate the man had shipped out from Conneaut, Ohio. The absence of the card surprised the reverend, who had assumed it would have remained with the body as it traveled to the Soo. Although an unscrupulous act by some individual eager to obtain a souvenir of the disaster may be the root cause of the artifact's disappearance, it is equally likely that it became lost during the cross-country journey.[28]

Reverend Easterday also told of a young fisherman who came across a second victim floating quite a distance off shore that was attached to a life preserver marked with the sunken vessel's name. Unable to pull the body into his boat, the fisherman attached a line to a life preserver band in an attempt to tow it to shore. This effort came to an abrupt end a short time later, however, when the band snapped and the corpse disappeared from sight before the young man could enlist help to recover it.[29]

Later that same day, another local resident, Clinton Endress, returned from Whitefish Point with information that contradicted a local rumor of two additional bodies being discovered in the search area. During a subsequent conversation with reporters, Endress related the prevailing belief among life-saving crews patrolling the beaches that the *D. M. Clemson* sank in relatively shallow somewhere offshore between the Crisp Point station and Grand Marais.[30]

As reported by the December 19, 1908 edition of Sault Ste. Marie's *Evening News*, articles from the lost steamer not only washed up on the Michigan coastline but were also found floating 21 miles northeast of Whitefish Point in Ontario's Batchewana Bay on the eastern shore of Lake Superior. With a number of life preservers bearing the name "Clemson" intermixed with this considerable amount of wreckage, little doubt existed as to its origin.[31]

With Captain Samuel Chamberlain being a thirty-second degree Mason, the Masonic Fraternity of Duluth offered a $100 reward for the recovery of his body, an offer extended to include six other members of the crew belonging to that order. A ring bearing a thirty-second degree emblem, the organization said, could identify the remains of Captain Chamberlain. Unsurprisingly given the lack of recovered bodies, the generous bounties (approximately $2,600 each in 2016 dollars) went unclaimed.[32]

On January 8, 1909, the friends and relatives of those lost in the sinking of the *D. M. Clemson* gathered in the auditorium at the Masonic Temple in Duluth to observe a memorial service arranged to honor not only its own members killed in the disaster but the crew as whole. Taking place just over one month after the sinking and some 300 miles away from the supposed location of the wreck, the ceremony did not have the deep sense of gloom normally associated with a funeral. As Reverend A. H. Wurtele recited the service associated with the burial of the dead at sea, however, several of those in the large room sobbed when he reached the line, "...when the sea shall give up its dead."[33]

With no survivors or eyewitnesses to its demise, the disappearance of the *D. M. Clemson* baffled those experts schooled in the design, construction, and operation of steel bulk carriers on the Great Lakes. A review of the steamer's service history during the last three months of its existence provides a tantalizing insight into some possible factors that may have contributed to its loss. Could the vessel have sustained heavier damage than initially thought when it hit the breakwater at Ashtabula on October 20, 1908? Although receiving temporary repairs immediately following the accident, the brief time spent in the harbor seems to preclude any thorough survey of the vessel's bottom in a dry dock. If the *Clemson* was operating with hidden hull damage, the grounding on Point Pelee just four days later surely could have magnified the seriousness of the structural defect.

Interestingly, just ten days before passing upbound at Sault Ste. Marie, Ontario for the final time, the *D. M. Clemson* encountered a heavy gale on Lake Superior while downbound with a load of iron ore for Ashtabula. After battling heavy waves and freezing temperatures for two days, the 468-foot steamer finally arrived at the Soo Locks coated in a heavy layer of ice. Although surviving the gale with little apparent damage, the stresses placed upon *Clemson*'s hull during this encounter would have certainly exacerbated any hull deficiencies stemming from the earlier Ashtabula accident.[34]

With a severely weakened hull, the possibility exists that the *D. M. Clemson* simply broke apart in the storm encountered just hours after it parted company with the *J. J. H. Brown* when both vessels passed Whitefish Point on November 30, 1908. Such a scenario explains the apparent rapidity of the sinking with most of the crew unable to abandon ship before it plunged to the bottom. During such a structural breakup, anyone trying to escape the foundering vessel would have little time other than to grab the nearest life preserver and virtually no chance to launch a lifeboat before ending up in the bitterly cold water. The absence of the lake freighter's lifeboats and a lack of bodies found during the recovery effort provide mute evidence to support this conclusion.

One theory circulating at the time of the disaster put forth the possibility of a power loss leaving the *Clemson* helpless in the storm while another explained the sinking with massive flooding through a sprung hull seam. Meanwhile, some marine observers attempted to draw a parallel between the loss and that of the steamer *Cyprus* in the same part of Lake Superior the previous year. Foundering in a storm on October 11, 1907, the end of this 440-foot steamer came only 24 days after its launch at the American Ship Building Company yard in Lorain, Ohio. In the case of the *Cyprus*, however, one sailor survived the wreck to tell of the vessel taking on water after losing some of its hatch covers to the heavy seas. Although the abundance of hatches recovered in the weeks following the sinking of the *D. M. Clemson* seems to suggest a similar sequence of events, it remains unknown if they came loose during the storm or blown off by an explosive build up of air pressure as the steamer dove beneath the waves. Furthermore, the newer overlapping steel hatches installed aboard the *Cyprus* had little in common with the *Clemson*'s traditional wooden hatches.[35]

Another aspect of the *D. M. Clemson*'s final voyage to garner considerable attention in the regional press was Captain Samuel Chamberlain's decision to pursue a southern course across Lake Superior during the autumn storm season rather than the less exposed northern course. As noted earlier, the shorter southern course exposed vessels to the full fury of northwest and northeast gales, while a ship sailing the more time consuming northern course experienced a less arduous voyage in the lee provided by the lake's north shore. The loss of the *Clemson* and the survival of the *J. J. H. Brown*, the latter of which took the northern route, led many to question why lake freighters did not take the northern course after the beginning of November. Lake mariners, however, were quick to point out that an overriding consideration influencing such decisions was the insistence of shipping companies to save time and, therefore, money.[36]

Six months after the *D. M. Clemson* sank, a group of Native Americans found the badly decomposed body of a man on the southwest corner of Ile Parisienne in the middle of Whitefish Bay. This news first reached Superintendent Ross of the Canadian canal at Sault Ste. Marie, Ontario on the morning of May 18, 1909 in a message from Joe John of the Goulais Bay Mission some fifteen miles north of the city. Missing one leg and lying on the beach exposed to the elements for a prolonged period, the remains amounted to little more than a pile of bones that bore the unmistakable scars of having been picked over by birds. Based upon the location of its discovery, the general presumption was that the body belonged to a crewmember of the lost steamer.[37]

Later that same month, Captain A. A. Batten of the Dominion Fish Company steamer *Caribou* came across some flotsam from the *D. M. Clemson* near Michipicoten Island and inside Batchewana Bay. Recovering at least two pieces of debris from the water, the crew pulled aboard a teak door and the blade of an oar clearly marked with the steamer's name. In addition, Captain Batten told of sighting a couple of oil barrels and the piece of a spar were among an assortment of wreckage he saw washed up on a beach in Batchewana Bay.[38]

Reports of its disappearance carried by newspapers across the nation, the *D. M. Clemson* was the largest ship lost on the Great Lakes during the 1908 shipping season. Unable to survive an encounter with forces beyond its control, the wreck of this steamer remains elusive on the bottom of Lake Superior.

On October 28, 1916, nearly eight years following the sinking of the *D. M. Clemson*, the American Ship Building Company at Lorain, Ohio launched the second ship to carry that name on the Great Lakes. Entering service early the following season, this 600-foot vessel incorporated the latest advancements in the design of lake steamers. Although only thirteen years separated their construction, the new steamer was able to carry a payload 80 percent larger than that of its predecessor.

Built for the United States Steel Corporation's Pittsburgh Steamship Company fleet, the *D. M. Clemson* (2) operated faithfully for the steel maker through two world wars and an era of great industrial expansion until laying up for the final time in 1975. Having retained its original name throughout its long career, this ship sat unused at Superior, Wisconsin until its sale for scrapping at Thunder Bay, Ontario in 1980.[39]

Chapter Seven
An Enduring Mystery

During the early years of the twentieth century, the Pere Marquette Railway began an effort to acquire the Canadian owned Lake Erie & Detroit River Railway. As this process neared its conclusion in 1902, the two companies entered into a traffic agreement that resulted in the Lake Erie & Detroit River Railway beginning a ferry service across the Detroit River between Windsor, Ontario and Detroit, Michigan. This same arrangement also led to Pere Marquette establishing a cross-lake car ferry service on Lake Erie. Although the railroad had operated rail car ferries across Lake Michigan for several years, this was to be its first foray to employ such vessels on Lake Erie.

In 1903, Pere Marquette and the Bessemer & Lake Erie Railroad formed the Marquette & Bessemer Dock & Navigation Company. Incorporated on April 2 of that year, the new firm assumed control of the assets belonging to Bessemer & Lake Erie's subsidiary United States & Ontario Steam Navigation Company, among which included the 300-foot long wooden car ferry *Shenango No. 1.* Having operated exclusively on Lake Erie since entering service in 1895, this vessel had the capacity to transport 26 rail cars.[1]

Just eight months following the creation of the

Marquette & Bessemer Dock & Navigation Company, on January 1, 1904, the *Shenango No. 1* became beset in heavy ice just outside Conneaut, Ohio while on one of its regular voyages between that city and Port Stanley, Ontario. Firmly lodged in ice near the harbor entrance, the car ferry remained stuck throughout the next two months until being destroyed by fire on the morning of March 11, with the loss of one life.[2]

The destruction of the *Shenango No. 1* prompted Marquette & Bessemer to order a new car ferry from the American Ship Building Company. Built by that firm's Cleveland, Ohio yard as hull number 428, this steel-hulled vessel measured 356 feet in length and 54 feet 6 inches in beam. With a depth of 19 feet 6 inches, this ship had the capacity to carry up to 32 rail cars loaded onto its car deck by four sets of tracks. With construction continuing at a steady pace, the shipyard launched the new car ferry on September 12, 1905. Named *Marquette & Bessemer No. 2*, the steamer entered service later that year.

With its operational headquarters located at Walkerville, Ontario, the Marquette & Bessemer Dock & Navigation Company operated a series of routes out of Conneaut to two Canadian ports on the opposite side of Lake Erie, these being Erieau and Port Stanley. With passages of these vessels bisecting the normal east-west shipping lanes stretching across the lake, this trade relied entirely upon the movement of coal exported to Canada. Not attempting to operate its ships on a year-round basis, the company's navigation seasons during these early years normally ran from March or early April to the beginning of January.[3]

Shortly after entering service, the *Marquette & Bessemer No. 2* became popularly known among the local citizenry of Conneaut as the "car ferry," while the company's only other vessel, *Marquette & Bessemer No. 1*, received the moniker "collier." Having entered service in 1903 and committed to carrying coal between Conneaut and Erieau, the latter vessel incorporated an unorthodox design incapable of transporting rail cars but one that permitted them to be pushed across an open stern and onto its deck to deposit coal directly into the cargo hold. Upon arriving at Erieau, the vessel's crew removed the rails and hatches to allow clamshell buckets to unload the coal before making the return trip across the lake in ballast. Widely spaced on each side of its car ferry-like stern, the twin stack arrangement of the *Marquette & Bessemer No. 1* prompted many lake sailors to nickname this steamer the "grasshopper."[4]

Powered by a pair of 2,280 indicated horsepower triple-expansion steam engines, the *Marquette & Bessemer No. 2* could make the 58-mile voyage across Lake Erie in approximately five hours. Fuel for the car ferry's four Scotch boilers was loaded through two separate coal hatches located on its car deck. With virtually no demand for passenger traffic existing on the steamer's intended routes, the Marquette & Bessemer Dock & Navigation Company made no effort to include any such quarters in its original design specifications. Nevertheless, the *Marquette & Bessemer No. 2* later received limited passenger accommodations.[5]

Staunchly built to handle the stresses of late season navigation, the design of *Marquette & Bessemer No. 2* nonetheless lacked a stern gate to prevent water from washing onto its car deck. Although not a standard design characteristic of Great Lakes car ferries at the turn of the century, the absence of such a feature left the stern open to wave action. While proving satisfactory during calm conditions, such a configuration made the vessel vulnerable to flooding by a following sea during stormy weather. To minimize this danger, the crew of the *Marquette & Bessemer No. 2* worked around the lack of a stern gate by keeping their vessel pointed into the waves during gale force conditions.

On the morning of Tuesday, December 7, 1909, an increasing wind sweeping across Conneaut heralded the coming of a major storm. At 6 o'clock that morning, the *Marquette & Bessemer No. 1*, under the command of Captain Murdock Rowan, nosed its way into the blustery conditions as it departed the northern Ohio port on one of its regular runs across Lake Erie. At about the same time, dockworkers began loading the first of 30 railcars aboard its fleet mate, *Marquette & Bessemer No. 2*, as the car ferry prepared to make its scheduled run to Port Stanley. This particular consignment consisted of 26 cars of coal, 3 cars of steel products, and 1 car of iron castings. Carefully balancing the loaded cars to prevent the car ferry from listing, this operation went smoothly and without incident.[6]

With its scheduled departure time drawing ever nearer, the delicate loading operation most assuredly drew the attention of the car ferry's master, Captain Robert Rowan Mcleod. At age 47, Captain McLeod was born to Scottish immigrants on October 3, 1862 in the sleepy village of

A dynamite charge explodes alongside the *Marquette & Bessemer No. 2* while the car ferry is stuck fast in ice on Lake Erie.

Kincardine, Ontario. Located on the shores of Lake Huron some thirty miles north of Goderich, the small community was home to a large number of mariners. Coming from a large family, five of Robert's six brothers were to find work on the lakes with two rising through the ranks to captain their own vessels. Robert McLeod went to the lakes for the first time at the age of twelve when he secured a position as a cook aboard the schooner *Maple Leaf* during the 1874 season. Two years later, he served briefly as a deckhand aboard the steamer *Ontario* before becoming a watchman two weeks later and wheelsman following the passage of another month. Serving in that capacity for the next seven seasons, Robert Mcleod sailed aboard the *Campana* in 1883. Rising through the ranks, he shipped out the following year as second mate of Canadian Pacific Railway's early steel steamer *Algoma*.[7]

Serving aboard a number of steam powered vessels over the next several years, Robert McLeod was appointed mate of the railroad car ferry *Ann Arbor No. 2* near the end of the 1891 season. Plying the waters of Lake Michigan on the ferry's normal route between Frankfort, Michigan and Kewaunee, Wisconsin over the following months, he gained considerable experience in winter navigation before becoming master of the steamer *Osceola* in the spring of 1892. Returning to the Ann Arbor car ferries at the end of the season, McLeod served as captain aboard the *Ann Arbor No. 1* during the ensuing winter. Sailing aboard the steamers *Colorado* and *Osceola* during the 1894 season, he brought out the former vessel at the beginning of the 1895 season before being appointed master of the United States & Ontario Steam Navigation Company's car ferry *Shenango No. 1* on October 1 of that year.[8]

A highly skilled mariner, Captain McLeod remained master of the wooden car ferry through the fleet's absorption by the Marquette & Bessemer Dock & Navigation Company before moving over to the *Marquette & Bessemer No. 1* in 1904. Over the years of his career as a shipmaster, Robert McLeod had earned the respect of his peers by demonstrating the ability to operate his vessel without significant casualty throughout all seasons of the year. This well-earned reputation obviously extended to the fleet's management as following the loss of the *Shenango No. 1*, they appointed him master of a replacement car ferry, the ill fated, and subject of this chapter, *Marquette & Bessemer No. 2*.

Serving as first mate was Robert R. McLeod's older brother, John, who had turned down a chance to command his own vessel in order to sail aboard the car ferry. The majority of the 32 crewmembers assigned to the *Marquette & Bessemer No. 2* made their homes in Conneaut. In an era without vacation time allowances, it was common for those employed on freighters plying the lakes to leave home in the spring and not return until the winter winds closed down the waterways between late November and mid-December. While railroad ferries operated a longer navigation season in comparison to their bulk carrying cousins, their shorter runs and regular schedules permitted their crews the rare opportunity of pursuing normal family lives.[9]

Although the crew managed to have the *Marquette & Bessemer No. 2* ready to sail in time to meet its scheduled 8 o'clock departure time that morning, the same high winds that its fleet mate had sailed into that morning had snapped the lines of ore carrier in the harbor. With the errant vessel blocking the channel, Captain McLeod had little choice but to await the arrival of tugs to clear his path from the harbor. Following a two-hour delay, the tugs managed to maneuver the freighter back to the dock, where it was to tie up for the winter.

As Captain McLeod waited impatiently for the tugs to finish their task, an individual named Albert J. Weis also found himself behind schedule as he rushed through the streets of Conneaut toward the ferry slip. At age 39, Weis had been born at Sandusky, Ohio and lived there until moving to Erie, Pennsylvania in his mid-20s. Engaging in the fishing business in that city, he eventually became treasurer of the Keystone Fish Company. It was in that role that he secured passage aboard the car ferry to conduct a business trip to Port Stanley, Ontario.[10]

With the channel now open, Robert McLeod wasted no time in ordering the lines cast off at approximately 10:25 that morning. As the *Marquette & Bessemer No. 2* began moving slowly away from the slip, several of its crew noticed a man running towards them shouting pleas to wait. Already behind schedule—a major inconvenience for a railroad car ferry—about the last thing Captain McLeod needed was the complication of a late passenger. With his vessel already in motion, the diligent captain was not about to bring the steel ferry to stop. Regardless, he allowed the stern of the steamer to drag along the dock so the tardy man could leap aboard. Now safely on board the *Marquette & Bessemer No. 2* and most likely short of breath, Albert Weis probably felt fortunate to be on his way to Port Stanley. As future events were to demonstrate, however, Mr. Weis would have been far luckier had he missed the ship's departure.[11]

Steaming past the safety offered by Conneaut's break wall, the *Marquette & Bessemer No. 2* nosed its way into a choppy Lake Erie as the wind rose in intensity. The increasingly blustery conditions also brought plummeting temperatures and heavy snows to the region. As the shallowest of the Great Lakes, seasoned lake sailors hold a special regard for the lake's vulnerability to having its waters stirred up by the slightest wind. Leaving the harbor in its wake, the delayed car ferry now faced the full brunt of the storm as it settled onto a northwest course toward the Canadian shore.

A short time after its departure, the *Marquette & Bessemer No. 2* passed the inbound *Alberta T.*, a commercial fish tug based at Conneaut. By this time, the freezing temperatures had deposited a heavy layer of ice on the small craft as it struggled to reach harbor. The captain of the *Alberta T.*, Frank Snyder, later reported that Captain McLeod tried to shout something across the waves with a megaphone when the two vessels passed but that the howling wind prevented anyone from understanding what he said. In light of the conditions facing the tug, Snyder and his crew made the assumption that the ferry's captain may have been asking if they required any assistance.[12]

By the middle of the afternoon, the wind had transformed itself into a raging southwest gale. With winds reaching 70 mph sweeping across the open waters of Lake Erie, the storm system threatened to destroy any vessel caught in its path. Continuing its downward spiral, the temperature fell to only ten degrees above zero. Perhaps the only fortuitous aspect of the gale was that there were relatively few vessels operating on the lake at the time as many had already been laid up at their winter berths. In addition to its assault against shipping, the storm also wreaked havoc on land by knocking down several power lines and blanketing northern Ohio and Pennsylvania with heavy snow.

On account of the storm, the failure of the *Marquette & Bessemer No. 2* to arrive at Port Stanley that afternoon initially generated little concern for the ship's welfare.

Believing the weather conditions convinced Captain McLeod it was unwise to attempt entering harbor, many assumed he might have diverted the car ferry to another port offering some protection from the wind. With each passing hour, however, the continued absence of the steamer only heightened fears at Conneaut that it had met with some calamity on the storm tossed waters of Lake Erie.

News of the car ferry's disappearance elicited a number of sighting reports from both sides of the lake. From Port Stanley, a Canadian customs officer claimed to have observed the *Marquette & Bessemer No. 2* attempting to enter harbor on Tuesday afternoon. Considering the ferry had departed Conneaut at half past ten that morning, the timeframe of this sighting corresponds closely with the vessel's standard five-hour crossing time. When the ferry called off the attempt to enter the harbor, it turned west in an apparent bid to reach shelter at Erieau. This same individual also claimed to have heard the *Marquette & Bessemer No. 2* blowing its whistle off the entrance to Port Stanley at 3 o'clock the following morning, an assertion corroborated by two other residents.[13]

Anchored off Conneaut due to the poor weather conditions, the captain and chief engineer of the steamer *Black* reported seeing the missing car ferry approach the harbor around midnight only to continue past the entrance on an easterly heading. William Rice, an operator of one of the harbor's Hulett unloading machines, told of hearing the *Marquette & Bessemer No. 2* sounding distress signals over a fifteen-minute period

95

between one and two o'clock in the morning. The dockworker described having heard the steamer repeatedly sounding its whistle four times and then five before returning to a series of four blasts, an observation confirmed by a coworker and another local resident. The simple fact that the *Marquette & Bessemer No. 2* made regular trips in and out of the harbor adds credibility to the account given by William Rice as it seems likely that the sound of the car ferry's whistle would have been familiar to anyone working or living near the docks.[14]

A further report came from a woman living east of Conneaut, who told of hearing the car ferry's whistle and observing its navigation lights from her home on Tuesday night. Upon first spotting the lights, she said, they appeared to be heading directly toward shore with the white masthead and red and green running lights clearly visible. Fearing the ship was about to run aground, the woman quickly put a light in her window. Apparently spotting the improvised danger signal moments later, the vessel took a sudden turn to port to avoid shore. The last the woman saw of the nighttime visitor was a single white stern light signifying the ship had turned back toward deeper water.[15]

As anxious families crowded the docks at Conneaut to await word on their loved ones aboard the *Marquette & Bessemer No. 2*, company officials offered words of hope by citing earlier examples in which the car ferry had gone unreported for several days during previous encounters with heavy gales. Despite the public display of confidence, however, fleet managers wasted little time in pulling the *Marquette & Bessemer No. 1* off its regular schedule to search the storm tossed waters for its missing fleet mate. Having itself gone unreported for several hours due to the storm, the 255-foot vessel probed the north shore toward Point Pelee before crossing the lake to cruise along the Ohio shore. Reaching Erie, Pennsylvania, Captain Rowan took his ship back across the lake and scouted the waters around Long Point. Following an exhaustive search, the small steamer returned to its regular run between Conneaut and Erieau without finding any trace of the missing car ferry.[16]

Three days after departing on its final journey, the first clue as to the fate of the *Marquette & Bessemer No. 2* came to light when the steamer *William B. Davock* of the Interlake Steamship Company passed through a field of wreckage off Long Point. Among the scattered debris, the crew sighted a green painted yawl—the same color as those carried aboard the missing car ferry. In a decision criticized by some regional newspapers over the following days, the *Davock's* master, Captain Benson Fox of Cleveland, Ohio, continued on course to his destination after failing to see any bodies and considering the seas too rough to recover any of the flotsam. Reporting his vessel's discovery to those ashore, Captain Fox sent the following wireless message:

> "The *Davock* has been running through light wreckage for about fifteen miles above Long Point. Abreast of Long Point we passed a metallic yawl boat painted green and full of water. We could not make the name."[17]

That same day, the Marquette & Bessemer Dock &

A view of the Conneaut waterfront catches the *Marquette & Bessemer No. 2* at its dock with full load of coal cars. Of note in this photograph is the absence of a stern gate at the rear of the vessel's open car deck. It is likely that the lack of such a design feature figured prominently in the vessel's subsequent loss.

Navigation Company contacted Charles N. Weis by telephone with a confirmation of his brother, Albert Weis, being a passenger aboard the ill-fated car ferry. Among the possessions the fish company treasurer had carried aboard was a suitcase said to contain $50,000 in cash to purchase a fish company in Canada.[18]

Near 11 o'clock on the morning of December 12, 1909, a lookout aboard the Pennsylvania Fish Commission's fishery tug *Commodore Perry* spotted a half-flooded yawl floating in eastern Lake Erie approximately 15 miles off Erie, Pennsylvania. Having searched the lake for two days, Captain Jeremiah A. Driscoll carefully maneuvered the steam tug alongside the wallowing craft. During the approach, the crew soon saw that the yawl contained the lifeless forms of several men frozen to death in their seats. Coming closer, they soon were able to read the words *"Marquette & Bessemer No. 2"* painted in large block letters on the bow of the boat just above the phrase, *"No. 4."* This left no doubt that the steam tug had located the No. 4 lifeboat from the missing car ferry.[19]

Fearing his men may capsize the semi-submerged craft during an attempt to remove the bodies in the still turbulent waters, Captain Driscoll had a towline attached to the yawl before beginning the slow trip back to Erie, Pennsylvania. With its flag flying at half-mast, the *Commodore Perry* steamed into port later that day with its gruesome find.[20]

An examination of the lifeboat revealed nine frozen bodies, eight of which were sitting in a variety of upright positions while another was lying encased in ice at the bottom of the craft. The removal of the bodies proved to be a delicate operation that vindicated Captain Driscoll's wise decision to forbid any such attempt out in the lake. Assisted by an improvised steam line from the USS *Wolverine* docked nearby, those assigned to the recovery operation had to physically chip the bodies out of the ice-laden yawl before transporting them to a local morgue.[21]

The lifeboat's occupants included coal passer Charles Allen, oiler John Hart, coal passer Ray Hines, coal passer William Ray, fireman Joe Shank, steward George Smith, porter Manuel Souars, fireman Thomas Steele, and second cook Harry Thomas. A search of the yawl revealed a complete set of clothing in the bow that apparently belonged to a tenth occupant of the boat that removed them before jumping to his death in the icy waters. The seemingly senseless act of removing clothing in freezing conditions is a phenomenon known to afflict certain individuals suffering from extreme hypothermia.[22]

The faces of the victims exhibited signs of bruising, presumably from slapping to keep blood circulating while awaiting rescue. With the exception of George Smith, who was found wearing an overcoat, the remaining bodies removed from the boat were clad only in workmen overalls. This suggested that the *Marquette & Bessemer No. 2* foundered quickly without adequate time for the men to dress in heavier clothing necessary to increase their chances of surviving the wintry conditions they could expect to face in the open lifeboat.[23]

An even more interesting discovery took place when the recovery team found two large knives and a meat cleaver on the body of George Smith. Why the steward had carried these items along when he entered the lifeboat created considerable confusion amongst examiners at the coroner's office, while also imparting yet another perplexing element to an already mysterious shipwreck.

Of the car ferry's three remaining lifeboats, one washed up on the Canadian shore near Port Burwell, Ontario. With no evidence of it ever have been occupied, the small boat most likely pulled free of the *Marquette & Bessemer No. 2* when it sank beneath the surface. Nearby, searchers found the floatation tanks of another lifeboat. The last remaining lifeboat remained elusive until the following spring when it turned up broken in two on a break wall at Buffalo.[24]

With the vast majority of those lost aboard the *Marquette & Bessemer No. 2* having made their homes in Conneaut, the sinking led to the cancellation of nearly all civic affairs in the city. For its part, the Marquette & Bessemer Dock & Navigation Company promised to cover funeral expenses for all of the bodies recovered. In addition, the company also paid a sum equal to one month's salary to each of the families of those killed in the sinking.[25]

Over the following days, funerals for five of the nine victims recovered from lifeboat No. 4 took place at Conneaut. This included funeral services for William Ray, Joe Shank, George Smith, Manuel Souars, and Thomas Steele. While the body of John Hart remained at Erie for burial in that city, that of Charles Allen was sent to Renova, Pennsylvania. Meanwhile, the company arranged to ship the remains of Ray Hines and Harry Thomas back to their respective homes in Canada.

The *Marquette & Bessemer No. 2* was not the only victim of the fall gale as the weather system also led to the demise of three other vessels. At the western end of the lake, the steamer *Clarion* caught fire after grounding on Southeast Shoal near the eastern entrance of the Pelee Passage. Although the steamer *Leonard C. Hanna* rescued six members of its crew, up to fifteen others perished in the blaze. To the south, a barge towed by the *Huron City* sank off Put-in-Bay with no loss of life. At the opposite end of the lake, stormy conditions forced the steamer *W. C. Richardson* (1) aground on Waverly Shoal near Buffalo, New York. Subsequently forced off the reef and capsized by heavy wave action, some sources indicate the sinking claimed five of the ship's nineteen crewmembers.[26]

In addition to these losses, the two-year old steamer *Josiah G. Munro* ran aground while attempting to rescue sailors from the burning *Clarion*. With losses amounting over $1,000,000 in vessel property alone, the storm caused at least 52 deaths on Lake Erie.[27]

A little more than two weeks after the *Marquette & Bessemer No. 2* sailed on its final voyage, a man named George Lawrence walked into the company offices at Conneaut on December 23, 1909. Originally believed to have been aboard the car ferry, he had missed the boat at Port Stanley on its second to last trip after Chief Engineer Eugene Wood tasked him with recruiting local men to serve as coal passers aboard the steamer. Sidetracked in this quest by a female acquaintance, he luckily missed the car ferry's departure and was therefore not aboard for the fateful return trip back from Conneaut.[28]

With the recovery of wreckage and victims from the disaster confirming everyone's worst fears, the search for answers shifted to determining the cause of the sinking. To many observers, the omission of a stern gate in the *Marquette & Bessemer No. 2*'s original design and construction provided a simple and credible explanation for its loss. Without such a structure, the vessel's car deck had virtually no protection from waves crashing over the open stern. Configured to carry coal gondolas, that deck had four openings through which massive amounts of water could find its way into the ship's lower compartments. This consisted of two hatches leading to the coalbunkers that were usually left open, and another pair leading to the engine room.[29]

Shortly following the sinking, a story surfaced that told of the *Marquette & Bessemer No. 2* nearly foundering in a storm about a month earlier when its stern fell into the trough of the waves. Although keeping the bow pointed into the waves during this encounter, the actions of Captain McLeod failed to prevent the car deck from flooding. Taking on tons of water, the car ferry took on such a heavy list that some of its upper rails slipped below the surface of the lake before the ship righted. In addition to speaking to his brother, Hugh, about this incident, Robert McLeod also related the details of the near sinking to company officials, who reportedly made plans to have a stern gate installed at the end of the navigation season.[30]

Put forth by the company's auditor, Alfred Leslie, another theory focused on the possibility of the railcars breaking loose from their restraints on the car deck. Free to move about from the tossing action of the rough seas, the sudden movement of the heavy cars may have capsized the vessel with little warning.[31]

Representing the most significant loss resulting from the gale that swept over Lake Erie during December 7-8, 1909, the *Marquette & Bessemer No. 2* was valued at $350,000 and its cargo estimated upwards of $40,000.[32]

At 2 o'clock in the afternoon of April 6, 1910, workers moving ice away from the powerhouse intake in the forebay of the Niagara Falls Power Company recovered the body of First Mate John McLeod. Found in a good state of preservation after floating in the lake for four months and wearing a lifebelt emblazoned with the car ferry's name, the body was fully clothed with the exception of shoes and socks. The local coroner, W. A. Scott, made the identification by examining documents recovered from the body that included an identification card, two postal money orders, tax papers, and a receipt for dues paid by John McLeod to the Conneaut council of the Knights of Columbus.[33]

It was exactly six months later, on October 6, 1910, that the body of Captain Robert McLeod was found lying on the lonely shores of Long Point. Exhibiting two deep gashes, the condition of the body led to considerable speculation concerning a possible connection between these apparent injuries and the mysterious existence of two knives and meat cleaver found in lifeboat No. 4. Was this evidence of a possibly mutiny aboard the steamer as its officers lost control of the crew when discipline broke down as the ship began sinking? It is not hard to imagine fear leading to panic as the men raced to reach the lifeboats even as death stared them in the face. If such a revolt took place, it surely represents an event unheard of in the history of shipping on the Great Lakes.

In the end, however, no reasonable proof exists to substantiate a connection between the knives recovered from the lifeboat and the cuts in the captain's body. Having floated in Lake Erie for ten months through all types of weather, could not the mutilated condition of Captain McLeod's corpse resulted from something as straightforward as an encounter with ice or the propeller of a small vessel? Furthermore, could the calamity of the sinking have caught George Smith in the middle of his duties in the galley? If so, is it not also possible that in a state of panic he simply carried the tools of his trade with him during the dash to reach a lifeboat?

Combing the same general area that Captain McLeod came ashore, searchers soon found the body of wheelsman William Wilson. In addition to oiler Patrick Keith and Chief Engineer Eugene Wood having previously come ashore at other locations, this discovery brought the total number of victims recovered from the wreck to fourteen.[34]

Shortly after the loss of the *Marquette & Bessemer No. 2*, the Marquette & Bessemer Dock & Navigation Company once again contracted the construction of a car ferry with the American Ship Building Company. Meanwhile, the company found a temporary solution to the sudden loss of capacity by chartering the *Pere Marquette* for the 1910 season. Operating on Lake Erie without incident, the *Pere Marquette* resumed its normal routes on Lake Michigan at the end of the year only to return on an occasional basis to meet increased capacity demands through the 1915 navigation season.[35]

Launched at Cleveland on September 3, 1910, the new car ferry incorporated a nearly identical design to its predecessor, a philosophy that extended to it receiving the same name. With construction proceeding smoothly, the *Marquette & Bessemer No. 2* (2) entered service on October 6 of that same year when it departed Conneaut for Port Stanley. Ironically, it was on that very same day that searchers discovered the body of Captain Robert McLeod. In addition to an enclosed pilothouse, the new steamer also carried wireless equipment—a safety measure the company instituted fleet wide. Most significantly, however, the new vessel incorporated a stern gate to provide an extra level of protection against heavy wave action.[36]

Adversely impacted by the Depression and increased competition from other rail routes into Ontario, the Marquette & Bessemer Dock & Navigation Company applied for permission from the Interstate Commerce Commission to abandon its last remaining Lake Erie car ferry route in early 1932. Quickly approved, the company ceased operations on February 13 of that same year. Dependent upon the coal trade, car ferry traffic remained active on Lake Erie on a small scale until 1958.[37]

Entering a period of extended idleness after the company abandoned its ferry operations, the *Marquette & Bessemer No. 2* (2) saw subsequent service as a display craft at the Great Lakes Exposition held at Cleveland, Ohio in 1937. After several additional years of inactivity, the Filer Fiber Company of Manistee, Michigan assumed ownership of the car ferry before reducing it to a barge in 1944. Sold to Captain John Roen of Sturgeon Bay, Wisconsin two years later, the barge was renamed *Lillian* in 1948. Roen employed the barge in both the pulpwood trade and various other projects around the lakes. In 1972, the Bay Shipbuilding Company acquired the *Lillian* for use as a work barge at its Sturgeon Bay yard. As such, the former car ferry was engaged in a number of shipbuilding projects carried out at that shipyard during the next ten years. Having reached the end of its useful life, the *Lillian* was scrapped at Menominee, Michigan in 1997.[38]

Despite a considerable number of claims that have surfaced over the years, the exact location at which the wreck of the *Marquette & Bessemer No. 2* rests on the bottom of Lake Erie has yet to be established. Some of the conjecture surrounding this mystery has focused on the belief that the car ferry sank during the afternoon of December 7, 1909 shortly after it was observed turning to the west off Port Stanley. If true, the wreck is laying somewhere between that harbor and Erieau. Although strengthened by an incident suffered by the *Marquette & Bessemer No. 2* (2) a few years after the sinking when it struck an uncharted obstruction while en route to Erieau, it disregards reports of the lost steamer's whistle heard off Conneaut and the sighting by the woman living east of the city later that evening. Assuming that Captain McLeod was attempting to find shelter from the southwest gale, the latter sightings provide a strong likelihood that the ship actually rests far closer to Long Point. Due to the bottom topography of Lake Erie, it is also possible that the wreck has sunken deep into the mud.[39]

Chapter Eight
A Twin Disappearance

During the final months of World War I, the French Navy contracted the Canadian Car and Foundry Company to build a class of naval trawlers at its Fort William, Ontario facility. Fitted out as single-screw minesweepers with the intention to clear German mines, each of these steel-hulled vessels measured 143 feet in length and 22 ½ feet in beam. These compact dimensions permitted an uncomplicated passage through the restrictive confines of the locks and canals that connected the Great Lakes to the Atlantic Ocean in the pre-St. Lawrence Seaway era. Offensive armament of this class consisted of a 100mm (4-in.) gun mounted at the bow and another at the stern. While the construction of these minesweepers at the head of the lakes roughly 1,200 sailing miles west of Montreal may appear strange at first, this decision was largely dictated by the lack of available building berths as coastal shipyards struggled to replenish both naval and merchant vessel losses suffered during the war.[1]

With Canadian Car and Foundry's building facility located several hundred yards inland from the banks of the Kaministiquia River, however, the company's management had to find an efficient method of moving the finished hulls from the plant to the river for launching. The solution was to install a set of tracks extending from the building berths to the river's edge. Riding upon a pair of cradles, each of the hulls moved down the rails to be launched stern first into the Kaministiquia, which itself empties into Lake Superior. With the multiple building berths arranged side by side, the twelve minesweepers went together quickly with the launch of the lead ship, and namesake of the class, *Navarin*, taking place in July of 1918.

Following in quick succession, the shipyard launched the remaining eleven vessels contracted to the French Government over the next four months. This included the *Cerisoles* and *Inkerman*, which first entered their element on September 25 and October 10 respectively. Although the war had ended on November 11 of that year, work on the minesweepers continued at a brisk pace to permit their departure from the Great Lakes before winter clogged the St. Lawrence River with ice. Rushing at their tasks, perhaps a little more quickly than would have been considered prudent under different circumstances, shipyard workers struggled to fit out the *Cerisoles* and *Inkerman*, and a third minesweeper, *Sebastopol*, as the month of November drew to a close.[2]

With the first brisk winds of winter already making their presence known in the northern Ontario community, there was little time to waste as the French sailors assigned to the naval trawlers toiled aboard their new vessels. Consisting largely of soldiers pressed into naval service with little or no experience in ship handling, the wisdom of employing these crewmen upon a lengthy journey anticipated to cross four of the five Great Lakes and the North Atlantic is open to question.

It was against this backdrop that the *Cerisoles, Inkerman,* and *Sebastopol* prepared to depart from Fort William to cross Lake Superior on the first leg of their maiden voyage to France. Perhaps in a case of the worst possible timing, this journey was to begin in November, a month notorious for its severe weather as heavy fall storms descend upon the lakes to herald the coming of winter. Respected by every lakes sailor, the relentless and unforgiving power of these storms has laid claim to many ships along with their entire crews. In fact, just a little more than five years earlier, on November 9, 1913, the 545 -foot *Henry B. Smith* departed Marquette, Michigan with a

In a scene captured during the closing days of World War I, this view portrays six of the French minesweepers built at Fort William, Ontario in various stages of final construction. The simultaneous loss of two of these wooden vessels during their delivery voyages remains one of the greatest maritime mysteries in the history of commerce on the Great Lakes.

load of iron ore only to disappear into the depths of Lake Superior a short time later with its 25 crewmen. Destroyed by the most devastating storm system to strike the Great Lakes in recorded history, the shattered remains of the steel steamer remained hidden in the dark depths of the northernmost of the Great Lakes until its discovery in 2013 following a century of lying on the bottom.

The task of commanding the small flotilla fell upon Captain M. Leclerc, who was to lead the voyage from aboard the *Sebastopol*. Although bestowed with the title of captain for the operation, Leclerc actually held the rank of lieutenant in the French Navy. Each carrying a complement of 38 men, the *Cerisoles* and *Inkerman* were commanded by Captain Etienne Deude and Captain Francois Mezou respectively, both of whom, like their commander, had received the nominal rank of captain in recognition of their postings for the trip.[3]

Just before noon on Saturday, November 23, 1918, the *Cerisoles*, *Inkerman*, and *Sebastopol* departed Fort William under calm weather. With wartime restrictions still in effect, however, the maiden voyage of these ships began without the usual fanfare normally reserved for such occasions. Setting course to clear Passage Island north of Isle Royale and with the *Sebastopol* in the lead, the three minesweepers ventured into the cold waters of Lake Superior. To ensure a safe passage down the lakes, the *Sebastopol* carried two experienced lake pilots whose job was to provide Captain Leclerc with navigational guidance. In addition, each of the two other minesweepers carried their own pilots with Captain John

W. Murphy of Buffalo, New York assigned to the *Cerisoles* and Captain R. Wilson from Collingwood, Ontario aboard the *Inkerman*.[4]

Choosing the shortest and quickest route to Whitefish Point on the eastern end of Lake Superior, Captain LeClec guided the trio of ships onto a southeasterly course that would take them across the middle of the lake. Having made slow but steady progress throughout the day, the ships ran into a fall storm just after 6 o'clock that evening. As the wind from the southwest increased in intensity, heavy seas began their relentless assault against the small craft. In an effort to deal with the sudden gale, Leclerc turned the flotilla south towards the Keweenaw Peninsula to meet the rising seas. Despite encountering periods of heavy snow, the lights of the *Cerisoles* and *Inkerman* remained visible to the men on the *Sebastopol*'s bridge.

While approaching the Keweenaw Peninsula five hours later, the *Sebastopol* nearly capsized after falling into the trough of the waves. Steering the minesweeper out of its dangerous predicament after taking over the wheel from the helmsman, Captain Leclerc headed northeast away from land. It was at this time that he lost sight of the *Cerisoles* and *Inkerman* in the darkness. Turning back to the southwest at midnight, Leclerc once again sighted his two traveling companions by observing their navigation lights. From this, he determined the vessels were sailing on a northeast course before their lights disappeared from view about an hour later. Making slow progress over the next few hours, the *Sebastopol* finally passed between Keweenaw Point and Manitou Island at 3:15 a.m. on the morning of November 24. Hugging the shoreline, the minesweeper succeeded in rounding the tip of the peninsula to anchor in Bete Grise Bay due south of Copper Harbor, Michigan, at half-past 7 o'clock that morning. All told, some thirteen hours had passed since the French minesweepers first encountered the storm.[5]

While anchored in their temporary refuge, the crew of the *Sebastopol* worked to clean up some of the damage inflicted by the storm. Along with battering the vessel's topside, heavy seas had caused some serious flooding in the engine room the previous evening before pumps managed to overcome the influx of water. In addition, the naval trawler had also suffered a steering gear failure and a defective anchor windlass. Although all three ships carried wireless equipment, considered state of the art at the time, radio operators aboard the *Sebastopol* were unable to establish contact with either the *Cerisoles* or *Inkerman*. With the personnel operating this equipment consisting of young men described as being little more than mere "students," however, Leclerc felt no real alarm over the silence of the two vessels. Although surprised the minesweepers did not find their way into the safety of Bete Grise Bay, he simply surmised the pair had continued on to Sault Ste. Marie, Ontario after losing sight of the *Sebastopol*.[6]

Having spent a little more than twenty-four hours in the bay, the *Sebastopol* departed its anchorage and steamed eastward to arrive at Sault Ste. Marie, Ontario during the early hours of November 26, 1918. Finding neither the *Cerisoles* nor *Inkerman* awaiting his arrival, Captain Leclerc asked the personnel operating the

Canadian Lock if the two ships had already made their passage. Receiving a negative response, he continued on the assumption that the missing craft and their 78 crewmembers were somewhere behind his own vessel and would most likely arrive at Sault Ste. Marie within a few hours. With the *Sebastopol* lowered to the level of Lake Huron, Leclerc decided to proceed without further delay. Before departing, the French naval officer put forth a request to have the arrival time of the two tardy vessels at the lock telegraphed to Port Colborne, Ontario, his next port of call.

Having traversed Lake Huron, the St. Clair River, Lake St. Clair, and the Detroit River before crossing the length of Lake Erie, the *Sebastopol* finally steamed into Port Colborne, where Captain Leclerc telegraphed his vessel's safe arrival to Lieutenant Garreau of the French commission at Fort William overseeing the minesweeper construction program. Expressing no misgivings about the two missing ships, Leclerc made no mention of the *Cerisoles* or *Inkerman* in his message, which Garreau received on December 1, 1918. After passing through the Welland Canal, the *Sebastopol* continued to Kingston, Ontario at the extreme eastern end of Lake Ontario.[7]

The first real concern for the missing minesweepers came on December 3, ten days following their departure from Fort William. Misled by Captain Leclerc's telegram and unaware of any unusual circumstances concerning the movements of the vessels, Lt. Garreau initially expressed doubts that anything unfortunate had occurred to the *Cerisoles* and *Inkerman*. The French officer went so far as to be quoted in early press reports as believing the

114

overdue ships were in fact with the *Sebastopol* at Kingston. Adding to the confusion was a veil of secrecy that shrouded the maiden voyage of the naval trawlers and numerous reports from upbound ships that had sighted the trio making good headway across Lake Superior. Furthermore, in the days before reliable radio communication it was a common occurrence for vessels to remain out of contact with the outside world for several days following a heavy storm. Factors such as these, led to early hopes that the *Cerisoles* and *Inkerman* were safely at anchor in some secluded bay or sheltering behind one of the many islands dotting eastern Lake Superior.[8]

On December 4, the tug *Bennett* departed Port Arthur, Ontario to conduct a search of the northern shore of Lake Superior in the hope of finding the overdue minesweepers. That same day, the tug *Sarnia* also sailed from that port to begin scouring waters around Isle Royale and the western part of the lake. Even as the tugs began their search, the United States Coast Guard began its own effort along the south shore. Meanwhile, commercial vessels venturing into the lake maintained an extra lookout for any sign of the small vessels or debris. Among those involved in the early hunt for answers was the package freight steamer *Huronic* of the Canada Steamship Lines' Northern Navigation Division, which scouted a number of islands in the search area.[9]

Leaving the *Sebastopol* at Kingston, Captain Leclerc rushed back to Sault Ste. Marie, where he arrived on the afternoon of December 5, 1918. His movements having come full circle since passing through the area nine days earlier, the French naval officer immediately set out to charter a tugboat to begin his own search of the largely uninhabited region of the Canadian shore. Following at least one unsuccessful attempt to secure a larger vessel, Leclerc managed to hire the 64-foot newly built and locally based tug *Frank Weston* captained by Samuel Shields. With winter tightening its grip on the region with each passing hour, Leclerc and the small crew of the *Frank Weston* departed on December 9 to spend the next six days searching the cold waters along the increasingly inhospitable north shore of Lake Superior. Finding no trace of the *Cerisoles* or *Inkerman*, Leclerc returned to Sault Ste. Marie, Michigan, the tug's homeport, empty handed.

In common with events of this character, the mysterious disappearance of the two naval trawlers sparked a number of false sighting reports. This included several rumors placing the minesweepers at various safe anchorages around Lake Superior. With several dozen lives at risk, searchers had little choice but to investigate these purported sightings regardless of their questionable nature. In the end, however, all of these hopeful, and often misinterpreted, reports proved to be false.

During the early days of the search, rumors concerning the overdue ships spread like wildfire through Fort William. Among the most outrageous were ones telling of the two missing minesweepers operating covertly on the lakes after conducting a secret passage through the Soo Locks. While seemingly plausible given wartime restrictions, this theory overlooked one basic question. Why advertise the disappearance of these ships after going to the trouble of orchestrating a clandestine voyage from Lake Superior? Furthermore, such an operation, by necessity, would have also entailed a secretive traverse of the St. Clair and Detroit Rivers and an equally stealthy transit of the Welland Canal and St. Lawrence River before the ships could reach the Atlantic.[10]

Another, more sinister, story claimed the *Cerisoles* and *Inkerman* had sailed from Fort William without any lake pilots aboard and that only the *Sebastopol* carried a qualified pilot to offer navigational assistance. This rumor asserted that the French sailing plan involved having the two missing minesweepers simply follow the *Sebastopol* as all three vessels made their way down the lakes. All went well until the trailing vessels lost sight of their leader in the storm. Under such circumstances, the inexperienced crewmen aboard the *Cerisoles* and *Inkerman* suddenly found themselves at the mercy of an angry Lake Superior without guidance and perished a short time later when their ships foundered. With no reason to doubt the official account of all three ships sailing with qualified lake pilots aboard, however, this tale has no basis in fact. As such, it represents just one example of the type of hearsay circulating through marine circles in the immediate aftermath of the disappearance.[11]

Despite the shroud of secrecy enveloping the movements of the French vessels, the superintendant's office at the Canadian Car and Foundry Company issued a statement on December 2 confirming the three minesweepers had sailed from Fort William nine days earlier. On December 6, an unmarked life ring came ashore 70 miles east of Marquette near Grand Marais, Michigan. The next day, some newly painted lumber also washed up in the same general area. The recovery of this debris followed the discovery a few days earlier of a cabin roof near Five Mile Point on the western shore of the Keweenaw Peninsula. Originally thought to have come from one of the overdue minesweepers, a subsequent examination of the cabin wreckage, however, quickly determined it had actually come from an earlier shipwreck.[12]

By far the most significant find concerning the lost ships, however, was a small boat recovered by a coast guard search party 25 miles west of Whitefish Point identified with the word *"Cerisoles"* painted on each side of its bow. Having traveled from Sault Ste. Marie to Grand Marais, Captain Leclerc and a representative from Canadian Car and Foundry concluded that the debris found near that small community did not originate from the missing ships. This fact notwithstanding, the French naval officer concluded that the boat found by the coast guard patrol came from the *Cerisoles* following a telephone conversation he had with the Two Heart River Coast Guard Station. Other than this diminutive craft, searchers found no other wreckage related to the two minesweepers.[13]

Returning to Sault Ste. Marie, Michigan following an exhaustive search that took him on a trek along Lake Superior's north shore and across the state's Upper Peninsula to Grand Marais, Captain Leclerc had little choice but to conclude that the *Cerisoles* and *Inkerman* had sunk with their entire crews. With the onset of winter weighing heavily on his mind, Leclerc knew the same cold winds already bringing ice to the upper Great Lakes would soon threaten to cease navigation on the St. Lawrence River. Departing the Soo area on December 17, the French naval officer hurried to rejoin the *Sebastopol* at Kingston.[14]

The lack of bodies and any substantial amount of debris clearly suggests that whatever happened to the *Cerisoles* and *Inkerman*, the two vessels must have foundered quickly. In fact, the only piece of wreckage attributed to the lost ships, the small boat from the *Cerisoles* recovered near Whitefish Point, most likely ripped free of its mounts as the minesweeper slipped beneath the waves.

Widely acknowledged as one of the greatest mysteries in the maritime history of the Great Lakes, the disappearance of the *Cerisoles* and *Inkerman* into the depths of Lake Superior has led to a considerable amount of speculation over the nearly one-hundred years since their departure from Fort William on that fateful voyage. One possible explanation for the disaster that cost seventy-eight lives focuses on the 100mm gun armament fitted to this class of naval trawler. Installed topside, the weight of the gun mounts may have created stability problems that made the sunken ships highly vulnerable to capsizing in heavy seas. Apparently perceiving the gun armament a serious stability threat, the French naval authorities ordered the mounts removed from the remaining minesweepers at Quebec City before allowing them to venture into the Atlantic.

With the three French minesweepers traveling as a group across Lake Superior, there existed a possibility that a collision could explain the loss of the *Cerisoles* and *Inkerman*. The apparent rapidity of the double sinking, however, casts doubt on this theory as such an event would have likely created a considerable amount of wreckage along with providing the crews a chance to escape the stricken ships. In addition, the reasonable assumption that the individual ships would have maintained a respectable distance from one another in the heavy sea conditions experienced that night makes the possibility of a collision seem remote at best.

One of the more curious theories to arise from this incident alleges the shipyard failed to remove several wooden pegs used as temporary fasteners during construction. These, as the story goes, failed from stresses placed on the hulls during the storm, thereby causing both naval trawlers to sink quickly. The lack of any evidence of such fasteners aboard the *Sebastopol* or any of the other identically built minesweepers, however, brings this hypothesis into question. Furthermore, despite the "no frills" approach their construction necessitated by wartime constraints, there is no reason to believe that the Canadian Car and Foundry Company took any critical shortcuts during the construction of these vessels.

In 1929, the charting of Superior Shoal in mid Lake Superior gave rise to speculation that this underwater formation may have been a factor in the loss of the *Cerisoles* and *Inkerman*. Reaching to just within 21 feet below the surface of the lake, a ship caught in heavy weather could easily rip open its hull by bottoming out on the shoal. Such damage has the potential to cause a sinking within a short time, which in the days before reliable radio communication may have gone unnoticed until the vessel became overdue at its next port of call. With the shoal located approximately 50 miles north of Copper Harbor, Michigan, however, it seems nearly impossible that the *Cerisoles* and *Inkerman* would have sailed roughly that distance north after Captain Leclerc lost sight of them near Keweenaw Point.

In light of the difficulties experienced by the *Sebastopol* during the storm, the most likely explanation for the loss of these two ships is that they capsized after falling into the trough of the waves. The suddenness of such a sinking goes a long way in explaining the lack of bodies and wreckage. In addition, a steering gear failure of a nature similar to that experienced by Captain Leclerc aboard the formation's flagship would have left the two minesweepers at the mercy of the waves, a situation they would be unlikely to survive. While the possibility exists that the *Cerisoles* and *Inkerman* met their fates in close proximity to one another, there is an even chance that these ships sank hours apart and actually lie on the bottom separated by several miles.

In the end, none of the French naval trawlers built by the Canadian Car and Foundry Company in 1918 ever made it to France on their delivery trips. Instead, they sailed to Boston, Massachusetts, where the French government placed them up for sale. By ocean standards, several members of this class went on to enjoy lengthy and active careers. While two of these vessels, one of which was the *Sebastopol*, operated for only 15 years, nearly one-half of this class survived well into the 1950s with the last unit, originally built as the *Malakoff*, lasting until 1974 when, as the *Illex*, it sank off Bay Roberts,

Newfoundland.

Entombed within the silent confines of an underwater prison, the twin wrecks of the *Cerisoles* and *Inkerman* patiently await the day of their discovery. Only then, perhaps, will the mystery of this tragedy finally be unraveled.

Chapter Nine
Sailed Away on Lake Erie

Belching a dense cloud of black smoke from its single stack, the wooden-hulled steam tug *Cornell* sailed past the harbor breakwaters at Cleveland, Ohio during the early afternoon hours of Thursday, December 21, 1922. While cold, the weather at the time was clear with just a touch of wind. Although frigid temperatures and the formation of ice across the Great Lakes had already sent most commercial vessels to their winter layup berths, those aboard the small vessel found the lake in a placid mood as they began their eastward voyage to Buffalo, New York. While appearing routine, the departure of the *Cornell* that particular afternoon was to result in one of the most mysterious disappearances on Lake Erie.

Built by the Union Dry Dock Company at Buffalo in 1888 as the *Grace Danforth*, this tugboat began its career as a member of the Hand & Johnson Tug Line of that same city. Measuring 72 feet in length and 17 feet 5 inches in beam, the 65-ton tug carried a crew of five. Based at the city of its construction, the *Danforth* operated year-round moving ships around the busy harbor. Among its tasks was the shifting of vessels that arrived for layup at the end of the season carrying grain storage cargoes to help alleviate the shortage of elevator capacity at the port over the winter months.

A search of the historical record reveals the Hand & Johnson Tug Line commonly employed the *Grace Danforth* to assist in breaking ice at Buffalo at the beginning of the navigation season. One such example took place on April 10, 1889 when this tug cut a path through the ice for the steamer *Owego* when that vessel made the first commercial departure from the harbor that year. A further instance occurred on March 30, 1897 when the *Danforth* began breaking ice at Buffalo in anticipation of the beginning of a new shipping season, an early arrival of which included the passenger steamer *City of Buffalo* later that week.[1]

In 1893, the *Grace Danforth* was in the process of pulling the barge *Curtis* off the rocks in the Niagara River when it lost its boiler after capsizing in the swift river currents. Requiring a replacement boiler, a new deck, and other major repairs amounting to a cost of just over $6,000, the tug departed the shipyard as a practically new vessel.[2]

The late 1890s was a time of significant change in tug and towing industry on the Great Lakes. In July of 1899, the Hand & Johnson Tug Line was one of several such companies involved in a major merger that resulted in the formation of the Great Lakes Towing Company. Established at Cleveland with a capital stock of $5 million and composed of several previously independent operators, the new company featured operations stretching from Duluth and Chicago in the west and across the lakes to Buffalo on the eastern end of Lake Erie. With its duties relatively unaffected by the consolidation, the *Grace Danforth* remained active in the Buffalo area.[3]

A little more than six years after becoming a member of

the Great Lakes Towing Company, the *Grace Danforth* was involved in the rescue of a disabled passenger steamer on a stormy Lake Erie. This occurred on August 15, 1905 when the sidewheel steamer *Idlewild* sustained a broken rudder in gale force conditions approximately twelve miles from Buffalo. At the time of the incident, the vessel was carrying 250 excursionists en route to Crystal Beach, Ontario.[4]

With his vessel at the mercy of the waves, Captain Joseph Loughridge ordered the crew to begin blowing distress signals. Alerted by the sounds of the pleading whistle blasts, the members of a canoe club located three miles southwest of Crystal Beach on Point Abino telephoned Buffalo with news of the steamer's plight. This resulted in the frenzied departure of a U.S. Life-Saving Service crew, several tugs, and the passenger steamer *Darius Cole*, all of which raced toward the last known position of the *Idlewild*. Among the vessels involved in this effort was the tug *Grace Danforth*.[5]

Fighting heavy seas, the life-saving crew managed to get a line aboard the rolling passenger steamer. This effort to render assistance came to an abrupt end when, moments later, the line snapped as the crew pulled its boat alongside. Arriving on the scene, the tug *Babcock* closed in and managed to secure a hawser to the *Idlewild* before becoming disabled itself when the line fouled its propeller. Unable to participate any further in the rescue effort, the *Babcock* returned to Buffalo in tow of the tug *Delta*.[6]

Undeterred by the previous failed attempts, Captain Cassin maneuvered the *Darius Cole* to within three feet of

125

the *Idlewild*. As the 400 excursionists aboard the *Cole* looked on, the crew managed to pass two lines to the drifting passenger vessel, both of which snapped. A third attempt by Captain Cassin came to an abrupt end when the stern of his vessel struck the bow of the *Idlewild* in a crash that resulted in bent hull plates and broken woodwork.[7]

Still floating helplessly in the heavy seas, the gale continued its assault on the *Idlewild*. Falling into the trough of the waves near Waverly Shoal, the strong winds toppled the steamer's stack. Careening overboard, the stack carried along approximately 30 feet of the hurricane deck as it plunged into the waters of the lake. Perceiving the danger of the stack's imminent collapse, Captain Loughbridge managed to avoid any injuries among the steamer's passengers by warning them to clear the area.[8]

About four and one-half hours after first becoming disabled, the *Grace Danforth* and *Conneaut* finally managed to put lines aboard the drifting *Idlewild*. Towed back to Buffalo, the damaged steamer disembarked its passengers before going to a nearby shipyard for repairs. Operating on the lakes until 1913, the *Idlewild* saw subsequent service as a molasses barge on the Erie Barge Canal until an accident led to its abandonment six years later.[9]

Renamed *Cornell* in 1907, the Great Lakes Towing Company contracted the reconstruction of this tug two years later. Remaining active in the towing trade on Lake Erie even as newer tugs assumed an increasing share of its duties, age and business conditions finally caught up

126

with the *Cornell* when it went into an idle status at Cleveland. Near the end of the 1922 shipping season, the Syracuse Sand Company of Syracuse, New York purchased the out of commission tug for use on the New York State Barge Canal. This transaction included the cost of both the *Cornell* and its delivery voyage to Syracuse.[10]

With winter threatening to close down the Great Lakes to further navigation, the *Cornell* departed Cleveland for the final time on December 21, 1922. The voyage to its new duties required a transit of Lake Erie to Buffalo, where the tug would enter the New York State Barge Canal. Carrying a double crew to facilitate its lengthy delivery voyage, the eight men aboard the tug included two masters, Harry Brault and Edward Kenneth along with a pair of engineers, William Gleason and William Mantell. The remainder of the vessel's complement consisted of Charles Crist, Thomas Hewitt, Michael Paytosh, and John Sieders. Hailing from the Cleveland area, all of these men were on the payroll of the Great Lakes Towing Company.[11]

Settling upon an easterly course after clearing Cleveland, the *Cornell* began its voyage in clear weather. Later that night, the crew of the tug *Charles A. Potter* sighted what it believed to be the eastbound tug proceeding on its voyage about three miles offshore between Ashtabula and Conneaut. If this vessel was in actuality the *Cornell*, those aboard the *Potter* were surely that last people to see the doomed tug as it never reached its destination.[12]

The failure of the *Cornell* to arrive at Buffalo in a timely manner generated little initial anxiety as most of those concerned held the belief that the tug had simply sought shelter from a system of heavy weather that passed over the lower lakes region on the day following its departure from Cleveland. By the morning of December 23, however, the continued silence concerning the whereabouts of the overdue vessel evaporated any remaining hope that the tug had not met with any misfortune during its voyage. Raising the alarm, the Great Lakes Towing Company dispatched the *Tennessee* from Buffalo and the *T. C. Lutz* from Cleveland. Retracing the *Cornell's* probable course across Lake Erie in opposite directions, the search by these tugs expanded with the arrival of two more of the company's tugboats, the *Q. A. Gilmore* and *Oregon*.[13]

The search received a significant boost when H. B. Shaver, superintendent of the U.S. Air Mail field at Cleveland, offered to dispatch three planes to Erie, Pennsylvania to scout the waters of Lake Erie between that city and Long Point. This arrangement was contingent on the positioning of tugs to guarantee the safety of the pilots in the event of an emergency. With little hope remaining of finding any survivors, the search of the lake continued through Christmas Day without result.[14]

While working a search pattern between Long Point and Port Colborne, Ontario at around 10 o'clock the following morning, a lookout aboard the *Q. A. Gilmore* spotted a yawl floating in the distance. Moving closer, the crew of the tug recovered the small boat approximately 15 miles off Port Colborne. Identifying the craft as belonging to the *Cornell*, this discovery came after the *Gilmore* had come across several oil cans floating in the lake about 10 miles west of the yawl's location. Inside the recovered boat, the crew of the tug found one lightly clad body wearing a life preserver. Encased in a heavy layer of ice, the body was lying face down against the wooden planks of the yawl's bottom. After remaining in the area for several hours in the hope of finding additional victims or debris, the master of the *Gilmore* set course for Erie, Pennsylvania.[15]

Upon arriving at that port, a crewman from the *Q. A. Gilmore* described the face of the body found in the yawl to marine reporters as exhibiting what appeared to be injuries from scalding. These statements created considerable speculation that the missing tugboat sank after suffering a catastrophic boiler explosion. Meanwhile, the extensive coating of ice forced recovery personnel to cut away one of the yawl's seats to remove the body to a local morgue. There, a search of the man's pockets produced documents identifying the body as that of Michael Paytosh. Furthermore, a more thorough examination of the remains revealed the facial discoloration was actually bruising caused by intense cold rather than fire or steam as earlier reports had suggested.[16]

Staying overnight at Erie, the *Q. A. Gilmore* ventured back into the wintry conditions on Lake Erie the following morning to resume its hunt for additional flotsam from the sunken tug. Although the recovery effort included aircraft and several motorboats in addition to the tugs dispatched by the Great Lakes

Towing Company, the lake failed to surrender any further trace of the *Cornell* before officials suspended the search operation several days later.[17]

As the investigation into the disappearance of the *Cornell* began at Cleveland on December 29, 1922, officials of the Syracuse Sand Company proved elusive that morning by avoiding their offices in the Onondaga County Savings Bank Building in downtown Syracuse. The loss of the newly purchased tugboat proved to be the second disaster to befall the company that year. Just six months earlier, on June 25, 1922, one the company's tugs was moving three cordite barges on Oneida Lake near Verona Beach, New York when a fire led to a series of explosions that killed one woman and caused widespread damage to several buildings. In addition, the blasts sparked a panic among several thousand people at a nearby amusement park.[18]

The lack of any survivors or significant amount of debris left those tasked with investigating the loss of the *Cornell* with far more questions than answers. Nonetheless, the recovery of the vessel's yawl and the body of Michael Paytosh provided some intriguing clues into the tragedy. The lightly dressed condition of the body suggested a sudden foundering but not so quickly that there was not sufficient time to don a life preserver or launch the small boat.

Despite having spent some time idle, the *Cornell* successfully passed an official inspection in August of 1922. Furthermore, Captain Thomas W. Gould, an inspector of hulls assigned to the Steamboat Inspection Service at Cleveland, declared the lost tug as being seaworthy with no reported defects prior to undertaking its final voyage. Although mariners on Lake Erie experienced some adverse conditions on the morning following the *Cornell's* departure from Cleveland, investigators did not believe weather was a factor in the sinking.[19]

One theory that garnered considerable attention was the possibility of a boiler explosion. While explaining the sudden disappearance and lack of survivors, such an event seems unlikely with the vessel having passed a thorough inspection just months before its loss. According to L. R. Cross, president of Syracuse Sand, the recovery of the tug's lifeboat disputed the likelihood of a boiler explosion. To support his position, Cross told reporters, "This lifeboat was carried over the boiler house. If the boiler had exploded, is there anyone who supposes that the boat would have been in perfect condition when found?"[20]

The company president put forth his own theory concerning the *Cornell* sinking by raising the possibility of the tug suffering a broken stern tube after fouling a log in its propeller. Such incidents, he claimed, were commonplace in canal operations but usually did not result in loss of life. Cross estimated that flooding in such a case could have sunk the tug within ten minutes, thereby permitting enough time for the crew to launch the lifeboat.[21]

Some experienced lake mariners explained the recovery of only one victim in the lifeboat by advancing the theory of the crew attempting to lower the small craft as the *Cornell* settled by the stern. At some point during this process, the yawl may have floated away as the crew wound up in the cold waters. This conjecture centered on the belief that as being one of the strongest aboard the ill-fated vessel, Michael Paytosh was the only member of the crew to accomplish the difficult task of pulling himself into the small boat.[22]

In the end, the absence of tangible evidence left an abundance of questions and a lack of plausible conclusions. Although an official investigation by the Steamboat Inspection Service concluded it likely that a fire destroyed the *Cornell*, the exact circumstances leading up to the tug's disappearance and the death of its eight crewmen remain a mystery to this day.[23]

Chapter Ten
Doomed on Lake Michigan

As the sun dipped below the western horizon during the early evening hours of September 9, 1929, the waterfront of Ferrysburg, Michigan reverberated with the sound of gravel flowing into the hull of a most unusual vessel docked along the shore of the Grand River just upstream of Grand Haven. With its hull showing the usual bumps and scrapes associated with an active and varied career, the vessel in question on this particular occasion took its name from a Native American tribe that proved especially friendly to early French explorers arriving in the East Coast region of the New World. As such, the *Andaste* had retained its name over the many years following its 1892 construction by the Cleveland Shipbuilding Company at Cleveland, Ohio. Built for the Lake Superior Iron Company, the unorthodox design of the *Andaste* incorporated elements of both the whaleback type developed by Alexander McDougall and a standard lake freighter. Measuring 280 feet 2 inches in length, the hull of this steamer featured straight sides that sloped above the waterline and a conventional bow. In a harbinger of what was to one day become standard on the lakes, but nonetheless relatively uncommon for steam freighters of the day, the vessel's cabins were located at the stern. Built along with a nearly identical sister ship, the *Choctaw*, the configuration of the *Andaste* was termed as a "monitor" design.

With a rated carrying capacity of 3,000 gross tons, the *Andaste* received its motive power from a 900 indicated horsepower triple-expansion steam engine built by the shipyard. Home ported at Ishpeming, Michigan, the steamer entered service a few months into the 1892 shipping season. Referring to its design as "a compromise between the 'whaleback' and the ordinary type," the *Starke County Democrat* of Knox, Indiana related the *Andaste*'s first cargo of 2,300 gross tons of iron ore in its June 3, 1892 edition. Deriving its information from a dispatch from Cleveland, Ohio, the paper described this initial payload as, "...150 tons better than a steamer of exactly the same dimensions of the old type carried on the same draught."[1]

The *Andaste* and *Choctaw* operated for the Lake Superior Iron Company until the Cleveland-Cliffs Iron Company of Cleveland, Ohio acquired both vessels in 1898. After becoming a member of its new fleet, the *Andaste* continued carrying iron ore from the upper reaches of the Great Lakes to the hungry mills fed by unloading ports on the lower lakes. Returning up the lakes, the ship often carried cargoes of coal to prevent expensive voyages in ballast. Other trades included the movement of pig iron and, when the need arose, an occasional load of grain into Buffalo, New York.

Adopting new fleet colors around the 1912 season, Cleveland-Cliffs began a policy of painting its vessels in a unique scheme consisting of black hulls, olive drab cabins, and black stacks adorned with a bright red "C."

134

While destined to receive few modifications over the next 72 years leading up to the company abandoning its shipping operations at end of the 1984 season, the new color scheme nonetheless created a problem for fleet managers when it came to applying these colors to the *Andaste* and *Choctaw*. With the impact of countless fragments of iron ore creating noticeable reddish-brown streaks down the sloped surfaces of their upper hulls as it rained down during loading and unloading operations, Cleveland-Cliffs decided to paint the hulls of these vessels a dark red to hide the unsightly stains.

During the 1912 season, the *Andaste* was involved in a minor accident on the St. Marys River. This took place on May 30 of that year when this ship attempted to pass the steamer *Randolph S. Warner* and its consort barge, *A. W.*

The steamer *Andaste* while operating for the Cleveland-Cliffs Iron Company.

Thompson, while all three vessels were downbound on Hay Lake. Upon realizing his steamer could not complete this maneuver before reaching a stretch of the river that prohibited passing, the captain of the *Andaste* slowed in an effort to fall back astern of the other two vessels. It was at this time that the port stern of *Andaste* veered into the starboard bow of the *Thompson*. A subsequent investigation into the collision ruled the former vessel at fault for the incident, thereby leaving Cleveland-Cliffs responsible for the nearly $9,900 worth of damage.[2]

In 1920, Cleveland-Cliffs contracted the Great Lakes Engineering Works to shorten the *Andaste* by 20 feet at its Ecorse, Michigan yard. The purpose of this reconstruction was to enable this steamer to transit the locks in the Welland Canal and those on the St. Lawrence River in response to a new coal carriage contract awarded to Cliffs by a customer with facilities located on Lake Ontario. At its new length of 260 feet 2 inches, the conversion reduced the vessel's carrying capacity by approximately 800 gross tons. By this time, however, the *Andaste* had become the last of the "monitor" vessels in the fleet following the loss of the *Choctaw* on Lake Huron five years earlier in a collision with the Canadian steamer *Wahcondah*.[3]

While operating in its new trade patterns, the *Andaste* suffered at least one minor accident when it ran aground off Carleton Island in the Thousand Islands section of the St. Lawrence River on November 25, 1922. This incident took place in heavy gale conditions while the steamer was loaded with 72,000 bushels of wheat and carrying a crew of 26. Going unnoticed by those on land, first word of the grounding came when a group of men rowed a small boat ashore to report the stranded ship's plight.[4]

In June of 1923, the Cleveland-Cliffs Iron Company and Leatham D. Smith of Sturgeon Bay, Wisconsin entered into a partnership with the establishment of the Andaste Steamship Company. Transferred into this new corporate entity, the *Andaste* underwent a conversion into a self-unloader at the Leatham D. Smith Dock Company at Sturgeon Bay. Near the end of July that same year, dockside tests of this newly installed equipment produced unloading rates twice that achieved by the shore-based traveling crane and bucket method. Although similar in principle to previous designs, Leatham D. Smith, the inventor of the equipment installed in the *Andaste*, boasted in newspaper reports that his system occupied only 25-percent of the space required by unloading gear used by other vessels at the time. In addition, Smith also pointed out that his design allowed a vessel to carry cargoes nearer to its center of gravity.[5]

During this same timeframe, the reconstruction of the *Andaste* into a self-unloading sandsucker prompted the formation of the Leatham Smith-Cliffs Company. Having served its purpose of facilitating this project, the completion of this conversion at the Leatham D. Smith shipyard in 1925 led to the dissolution of this firm.[6]

Incorporating a large steel A-frame structure and its associated belt housing extending up from the cargo hold near its bow, the new unloading equipment drastically changed the appearance of the *Andaste*. Below the high A

Although partially obscured by the passing steamer *I. W. Nicholas*, this busy harbor scene at Buffalo, New York provides a view of the *Andaste*'s stern configuration.

-frame, a long slender unloading boom extended aft toward the front the stern mounted cabins. Suspended by steel cables and capable of swinging to either side of the vessel, the boom deposited the steamer's cargo to any point on land within its reach without the need of shore side assistance. Although some observers may have considered the unloading equipment unsightly in comparison to the uncluttered appearance of a standard straight deck bulk carrier, it nonetheless extended the operational life of the aging steamer.

On the evening of Wednesday, November 17, 1926, the *Andaste* was one of several ships caught in a gale on Lake Michigan. Having departed Muskegon, Michigan under the command of Captain Frank Savage earlier that afternoon, the failure of the steamer to arrive at

Milwaukee, Wisconsin in a timely manner created considerable concern for its safety. It was not until the late hours of the following day that the *Andaste* sailed into Sturgeon Bay. Recounting his experiences over the past day and a half to anxious marine reporters, Captain Savage told of encountering a fierce storm in mid-lake and heavy seas off Milwaukee before setting course of Sturgeon Bay. At the time of this particular voyage, the *Andaste* was carrying a crew of twenty-four men and one woman.[7]

In 1928, the Construction Materials Company of Chicago, Illinois entered into a charter agreement to operate the *Andaste* in delivering aggregates to its dock on the busy Calumet River. Skippered by newly appointed Captain Albert L. Anderson of Sturgeon Bay, the steamer continued plying familiar waters by loading cargoes of gravel, sand, and crushed stone at various ports around Lake Michigan.[8]

In January of 1929, Leatham D. Smith informed Cleveland-Cliffs of his intention to sell his share in the Andaste Steamship Company. At the same time, Smith entered into an arrangement to settle various patent agreements in connection to the unloading gear installed in the *Andaste*. Concluded by the spring of that same year, this transition left Cleveland-Cliffs, Samuel Mather, and Albert Schneider as owners of the vessel.[9]

Shortly afterwards, Cleveland-Cliffs entered into talks to sell the *Andaste* to the Construction Materials Company. With the steamer having proven successful in its charter arrangement since the previous season, these negotiations reached a favorable conclusion with the construction supply firm agreeing to purchase the 37-year old vessel for $125, 000.[10]

As dockworkers at Ferrysburg loaded the last of the gravel cargo aboard the *Andaste* on the evening of September 9, 1929, Captain Albert L. Anderson toiled at making final preparations for the overnight trip across Lake Michigan. Ordering his crew to cast off the mooring lines, the experienced shipmaster began maneuvering his vessel up the Grand River towards the lake. Having operated on a schedule of making regular trips between the Michigan port and South Chicago each week that season, it is unlikely that the steamer's departure in the gathering darkness elicited any undue attention. During the approximately 3-mile journey from the loading dock to the harbor entrance, Captain Anderson almost certainly observed the small craft warning pennant flying at the Grand Haven Coast Guard Station in response to an advisory issued by the weather bureau earlier that afternoon. While the twenty-five crewmembers aboard the steamer could expect some blustery conditions on their cross-lake trek, such warnings forecasted less than gale force conditions that should pose no significant danger to a vessel the size of the *Andaste*.

While appearing routine, this particular voyage was to signify a change in ownership for the *Andaste*. Efforts to conclude the previously stated purchase agreement had resulted in the scheduled transfer of the steamer's title of ownership to the Construction Materials Company in the middle of Lake Michigan.[11]

At the Grand Haven Coast Guard Station, George Van Arkel observed the *Andaste* pushing its way toward the open waters of Lake Michigan. Noting this passage, he recorded the steamer passing through the harbor piers at precisely 9:03 that evening. Leaving the safety of the harbor in its wake, the *Andaste* settled onto a southwest course toward the entrance of the Calumet River at the southern extreme of the lake just southeast of downtown Chicago.[12]

About an hour later, the wind suddenly shifted and picked up in intensity as it grew into a strong northwest gale. Even as the *Andaste* sailed into Lake Michigan on that fateful night, a bulletin issued by the weather service predicting the onset of the storm was working its way through the bureaucratic channels necessary for it to reach the Grand Haven Coast Guard Station. As a result, personnel at the station did not post the required gale warning flags until two hours after the steamer's departure.[13]

Shown a year before its loss, this low quality photograph captures the modified appearance of the *Andaste* following the installation of its topside self-unloading equipment.

141

Considering the conditions experienced by mariners the previous night on Lake Michigan, the failure of the *Andaste* to arrive at the Construction Materials Company's dock on the morning of September 10, 1929 probably caused little concern. Did not the steamer survive a similar storm just two years earlier before showing up safely at Sturgeon Bay? With this precedent in mind, it is likely that personnel in the company's marine operations department simply assumed the ship had sought shelter in some safe harbor or was slowly making its way toward the Calumet River.

As the hours passed, however, the continued absence of the *Andaste* kindled a growing sense that something untoward had taken place. In the end, the steamer never reached its intended destination, or any other port for that matter. Overwhelmed by the early autumn storm, the converted self-unloading sandsucker simply vanished into the mysterious depths of Lake Michigan.

Confident that Captain Anderson had sought shelter in one of the many harbors around the southern shore of Lake Michigan, officials at the Construction Materials Company delayed in making a formal report of their missing freighter to the authorities for nearly two full days. During the intervening period, the company made numerous inquiries to regional coast guard stations in the hope of ascertaining the whereabouts of the *Andaste*. Unfortunately, this effort produced a number of erroneous sighting reports that placed the ship safe at various locations. Despite the reassuring tone provided by such scraps of information, the company remained skeptical to the point of chartering an aircraft to search the lower section of Lake Michigan on Wednesday afternoon. Covering a considerable portion of the lake over several hours, the aerial search ended without sighting the missing vessel.

With the *Andaste* remaining elusive on the morning of Thursday, September 12, nearly forty-eight hours after missing its scheduled arrival, company managers had little choice but to enlist additional aid in determining the fate of their vessel. That same morning, the search operation expanded as several craft ranging from coast guard patrol boats to private vessels began scouring the lake for any sign of the *Andaste* or its twenty-five crewmembers. Perhaps somewhat understandable during an era in which lake freighters often went missing for protracted periods following a major storm, the Construction Materials Company nonetheless received some harsh public criticism for its delay in reporting its overdue steamer.

Within hours, the search effort grew to include hundreds of small craft from several Michigan ports, with vessels putting out to Lake Michigan from Benton Harbor, Grand Haven, Holland, and South Haven. From Chicago, three coast guard vessels and the steel yacht *Mizpah* under the command of Captain McDonald also joined the search. Further assistance from the Chicago area came from four U.S. Navy seaplanes.[14]

By Friday, four days after George Van Arkel watched the *Andaste* clear Grand Haven for the final time, the first pieces of wreckage began drifting ashore on beaches between that city and Holland to the south. Among the scattered debris found along the shoreline that day was the steamer's pilothouse.[15]

Later that same day, the commercial fish tug *Bertha G.* sailed into Grand Haven carrying a grim cargo of wreckage recovered from the lake. Skippered by Captain George Van Hall, the tug came across the flotsam over a wide area stretching several miles in length some fourteen miles offshore and forty miles south of Grand Haven. Despite finding a considerable amount of debris, the crew of the *Bertha G.* saw no evidence of any bodies. The wreckage included a cabin door and some woodwork identified as originating from Captain Albert Anderson's office by Joseph Collins and George Evans. As members of the sunken vessel's regular crew, these two men had been fortunate in not being aboard for the ill-fated trip.[16]

On Saturday, September 14, the Construction Materials Company dispatched its tugs *Freedom* and *Liberty* to join the ongoing search. Sailing into Lake Michigan, the two tugs retraced the missing steamer's normal 114-mile course between Grand Haven and South Chicago.[17]

Meanwhile, further wreckage continued coming ashore. Near the mouth of the Sheldon Channel some nine miles north of Holland, F. H. Hulbert, a Port Sheldon contractor, discovered the piece of a wrecked cabin bearing the name *Andaste*. A few miles south, the caretaker of Wild Goose Beach found the vessel's nameboard along with a hatch cover, pieces of the vessel's cabin, and a pair of oars. Other items recovered from the lake included a desk belonging to the chief engineer and several letters addressed to those aboard the vessel at the time of its sinking. Many of these correspondences soon began appearing on display at various retail establishments around Holland, where they became objects of morbid curiosity. While mostly concentrated in the Holland area, some wreckage washed up as far south as Saugatuck, where searchers found a lifebuoy emblazoned with the vessel's name.[18]

The scattered remains of the *Andaste* prompted a strange migration of souvenir hunters to descend upon the coast of southwestern Michigan. Coming from as far away as Grand Rapids and a wide range of other communities in the western part of the state, a considerable number of men, women, and children scoured the beaches to gather any relics of the sunken ship they could lay their hands on.[19]

Intermingled amongst the wide assortment of debris, several of those lost in the sinking of the *Andaste* also slowly made their way to shore. Peering through a pair of binoculars while standing atop a sand dune near Castle Park on the afternoon of Saturday, September 14, John Kuipers, a deputy sheriff from Holland, spotted a body floating about 500 feet offshore. Recovered by Kuipers and two companions, the first victim pulled from the cold waters of Lake Michigan proved to be Second Engineer Ralph Wiley of Benton Harbor, Michigan. Found wearing a cork life jacket, the body had also been kept afloat by two life rings tightly attached with straps. Shortly following their grim discovery, the men arranged to have the body transported to a funeral home in nearby Holland.[20]

Later that same day, the body of First Mate Charles Brown washed up on a beach near Holland. Fully clad

145

with rubber boots, Brown's body was not wearing a lifebelt. Notified of this discovery, a crew from the Holland Coast Guard Station under the command of Captain S. J. Tost transported the body back to that city. A resident of Grand Haven and survived by a wife and two stepchildren, the *Andaste*'s first mate had previously been aboard the car ferry *Milwaukee* (3) when that steamer went missing for fifty-six hours following a storm on Lake Michigan in 1923.[21]

As additional bodies made their way onto area beaches, searchers found the remains of Captain Albert L. Anderson on September 16, about two miles south of Grand Haven. Like First Mate Charles Brown, the body of the *Andaste*'s master was not wearing a lifebelt. Representing just one of the seven bodies pulled from the lake that day, the discovery of Captain Anderson brought the number of victims recovered from the shipwreck to ten.[22]

Over a period extending into several weeks, searchers eventually recovered sixteen of the twenty-five crewmembers killed in the sinking. The bodies provided mute testimony as to the steamer's final hours. With the majority of the victims found to be wearing lifebelts, it seems likely that the crew had some forewarning of an impending disaster before the *Andaste* succumbed to the waves. During his examination of the remains, Ottawa County Coroner Gilbert Vandewater found that at least one of the victims had died from the effects of an explosion rather than by drowning. Such a finding suggests the vessel's hot boilers may have exploded when cold water flooded its engine room.[23]

146

While the list of the twenty-five crewmen lost on the *Andaste* included many lifelong sailors, the youngest person aboard the vessel was fourteen-year-old Earl Zietlow. Said to be big for his age and hailing from Grand Haven, this was the young man's first trip. Interestingly, Earl Zietlow obtained his position in the vessel's galley through Joseph Collins, a wheelsman who had been on vacation at the time of the ill-fated trip and, as previously stated, was to play a role in identifying recovered debris.[24]

Even as bodies and wreckage continued to float ashore, work had already begun to reconstruct the *Andaste*'s final voyage. News of the lost steamer produced a considerable number of sighting reports. One such account came from John Swift, who reported seeing the lights of a ship close to shore between Grand Haven and Holland at around 1 a.m. on the night of the storm. Watching the unknown vessel from his cottage, Swift claimed the lights remained in the area for approximately three hours.[25]

Personnel assigned to the U.S. Coast Guard station at Holland reported having spotted the lights of a vessel between 2 and 4 a.m., but did not observe any distress signals. Corroborated by a number of local residents living along the shore, this sighting led to the belief that the *Andaste* may have been trying to seek shelter at Holland. With the vessel having delivered gravel to the Harrington Dock at Virginia Park on numerous occasions during the previous season, its crew would have been familiar with the harbor. This left many to wonder if, in the moment of need, Captain Anderson attempted to seek the safety of Holland only to find conditions that precluded a safe passage through the harbor piers. If the ship spotted that night was in fact the *Andaste*, the lack of distress signals suggests that Captain Anderson felt his ship was in no immediate danger and was simply seeking to find shelter from the storm.[26]

With the storm producing winds reaching 60 miles per hour, the freight and passenger steamer *Alabama* was one of the many vessels caught in the sudden tempest. Shortly after 1 a.m., Captain Crawford and his first mate spotted the lights of another ship to the west and north of their own that appeared to be on a westbound course. Although unable to ascertain if the nameless vessel was under power, neither man saw any signs of it encountering any difficulty. In addition, Captain Crawford told of sailing the *Alabama* into Grand Haven at 4:43 that morning after deciding it too risky to attempt entering Holland or Muskegon.[27]

Another report came from Joseph Dunlevy, first mate of the steamer *City of Grand Rapids*, who claimed to have seen a set of lights resembling those of the *Andaste* in mid-lake as his vessel made one of its routine overnight trips across Lake Michigan. Observing the lights swaying wildly, he said the ship appeared to be heading toward land for protection even as it rolled heavily in the rough seas. Although believing it was experiencing some serious difficulty, Dunlevy claimed the laboring vessel displayed no distress signals.

With contemporary newspaper accounts reporting this encounter as taking place on Tuesday night, or nearly 24 hours after the *Andaste* is thought to have sank, some historians have chosen to disregard this sighting. A search of local newspapers during the week in question, however, reveals the southern half of Lake Michigan experienced a period of fair weather immediately following the gale of Monday night and Tuesday morning. By specifically stating, "A gale was blowing and a high sea running," it appears that Dunlevy's observations almost certainly took place during the storm and not the following night when the weather was markedly calmer. Could an anxious marine reporter have simply misquoted the first mate of the passenger steamer? If so, Dunlevy's observations assume a higher level of credibility. With both the *City of Grand Rapids* and the *Andaste* being committed to the Lake Michigan trade along the same general trade routes, it seems probable that Joseph Dunlevy would have been familiar with the ill-fated vessel. Therefore, it is also reasonable to assume he would have known any peculiarities that made the lights of the self-unloading sandsucker distinctive from other ships at night.[28]

Within days of the sinking, rumors alleging that the lifeboat davits on the *Andaste* had rusted to the point of becoming inoperable began circulating within marine circles. These assertions led to speculation that the crew was unable to launch the lifeboats as the ship foundered. The absence of the lifeboats amongst the wide accumulation of recovered wreckage combined with the evidence of the crew apparently having sufficient forewarning of impending disaster to don lifesaving gear provides support for the defective davit theory. Of steel construction and incorporating floatation chambers, there can be little doubt that the lifeboats remained tightly secured to their launching gear as the steamer plunged to the bottom.[29]

Hugh P. Mulligan of the Steamboat Inspection Service office at Grand Haven vehemently disputed such claims. Declaring he found no problems aboard the *Andaste* while conducting a preseason survey at Ferrysburg on April 22 of that year, Mulligan expressed his doubts as to whether the davits could have rusted so badly within the intervening time.

Others, however, remained unconvinced. One such individual was a member of the coast guard contingent at Holland named John Van Ingen. Having sailed aboard the *Andaste* earlier that season, a local newspaper quoted him as saying, "...the davits became rusty and unusable," between the April inspection and when he left the ship at the beginning of July.[30]

Other early rumors questioned the reliability of the *Andaste*'s powerplant. At least one of these stemmed from remarks purportedly made by Second Engineer Ralph Wiley to Mrs. Marie Nash, from whom he had rented a room in her Benton Harbor home since 1927. In their conversations, Mrs. Nash claimed Wiley had complained about the steamer suffering several engine breakdowns in mid-lake, some of which lasted 2-3 hours in length. She also told of the seasoned engineer expressing his reluctance to sail on what became the *Andaste*'s final voyage, including a frustrated moment in which he referred to the steamer as an unsafe "old tub."[31]

The spate of engine troubles reportedly suffered by the *Andaste* seems to have also caused some concern for First

Mate Charles Brown, who confided the ship's difficulties to his wife. Despite these reports, the ship successfully passed a survey by steamboat inspectors during a dry-docking at Chicago in June of that year. In addition, the Johnson Boiler Works of Ferrysburg performed a $28,000 refit on the steamer during the previous winter layup period. As such, there appears to be no real evidence of the *Andaste* being in anything other than good mechanical condition during the months leading up to its loss.[32]

If the ship did in fact lose power during the storm, however, it would have been at the mercy of the gale without the ability to maneuver. In such a precarious condition, it could have easily fell into the trough of the waves and swamped by the heavy seas.

Immediately following the sinking, several observers attempted to draw a parallel between the loss of the *Andaste* and the disappearance of the steamer *Clifton* in Lake Huron during an early autumn storm on September 22, 1924. Although the two ships shared several similarities, including both receiving self-unloading conversions at the Leatham D. Smith Dock Company, they were in actuality built to very different design specifications. Despite being widely reported in contemporary accounts of the disaster as sister ships, the *Andaste*'s "monitor" design incorporated only certain elements of Alexander McDougall's unique whaleback method of ship construction. In contrast, the *Clifton*, built at West Superior, Wisconsin in 1892 as the *Samuel Mather* (2), was a true whaleback embodying every aspect of that pioneering, but ultimately short lived, design philosophy. While a direct comparison between the two vessels is impossible, their losses just five years apart under similar circumstances certainly brings possible stability issues associated with the addition of the topside unloading gear into question.

Further evidence of possible stability concerns came from several sailors that previously served aboard the lost ship. One, Gerald H. Burg, of Benton Harbor told of the *Andaste*'s tendency to roll and pitch in heavy weather even while carrying a full load. A former deckhand from Chicago named Louis Broucek said the ship's tendency to roll often shifted its cargoes, a potentially dangerous situation that required the crew to enter the cargo hold and manually trim the load. With many sailors having grown fearful of the converted sandsucker, he added, the ship's officers had trouble recruiting a full crew.[33]

As related earlier, the Construction Materials Company received a considerable amount of criticism in its failure to raise the alarm for their missing vessel until it became two days overdue at South Chicago. Speaking to the press, Ottawa County Prosecutor Clarence Lokker stated his belief that an earlier official search effort may have saved some of the lost steamer's crew. He based this opinion on the discovery that the first victim recovered, Ralph Wiley, appeared to have been dead for only a short time when he was found. Furthermore, the lack of water in the lungs suggested the man died of exhaustion rather than drowning.[34]

Although a closer examination by Coroner Vandewater confirmed Wiley had died of exposure, it also revealed that death had taken place at least three days before a search party pulled his body from the lake. This finding presented the possibility of the man having survived for several hours in the lake following the sinking. It also reaffirmed the assumption that the delay of the vessel's owners in seeking outside help significantly decreased the possibility of finding any survivors.[35]

Well known among the local sailing community, Ralph Wiley had previously sailed as a fireman aboard the Benton Transit Company's passenger and package steamer *Bainbridge*. In fact, he was a member of the crew that brought the 152-foot long vessel to Benton Harbor from East Boothbay, Maine to begin its career in the Lake Michigan trade. Leaving a wife and five children back at his home in Maine, county officials arranged to ship Wiley's body back east for burial following a funeral service held at Grand Haven.[36]

Eight days after the *Andaste* embarked upon its final voyage, two men searching for bodies along a beach near Holland came across a piece of a board apparently coming from the lost ship. Scrawled across this fragmented piece of wreckage was the following message: "Worst storm I have ever been in. Can't stay up much longer. Hope we're saved."

Endorsed with initials corresponding to those of Captain Albert L. Anderson, this discovery led many to speculate that the master of the doomed ship had penciled the message. Coroner Gilbert Vandewater claimed to have no doubt in his mind concerning the authenticity of the message. Several steamboat inspectors and officials from other agencies connected with investigating the tragedy, however, remained unconvinced. Pointing out that the steamer carried a specially designed copper message case for use in just such an emergency and the improbability of Captain Anderson scribbling the note while fighting to stay alive in the rough seas, the inspectors concluded this find represented nothing more than a hoax.[37]

Under the direction of Coroner Gilbert Vandewater and County Prosecutor Clarence A. Lokker, a coroner's inquest into the sinking of the *Andaste* began at the Ottawa County Courthouse in Holland on the morning of September 24, 1929. The jury selected for this proceeding consisted of local business owners Fred Beeukes, E. B. Stephan, William Vissers, Henry Winters, Wynand Wychers, and its foreman, Mayor Ernest C. Brooks.[38]

After hearing several hours of testimony given by twenty-two witnesses ranging from company officials and meteorologists to steamboat inspectors and masters of other lake vessels caught in the storm that night, the six-member jury rendered its verdict on the evening of October 2, 1929. Absolving the crew of the *Andaste* of any blame for the sinking, the verdict also declared the steamer as being seaworthy and equipped with all of the appropriate lifesaving devices of the day. In addition, the jury also commended the Construction Materials Company, and the U. S. Coast Guard stations at Grand Haven and Holland for their tireless efforts in searching for the missing vessel and its crew.[39]

The loss of twenty-five lives aboard the *Andaste* came just a little more than two months following the Fourth of July drowning of ten beachgoers caught in an undertow at Highland Park Beach near Grand Haven.[40]

The 1929 shipping season proved particularly unkind to

mariners on Lake Michigan. This was especially true for the month of October of that year in which three ship losses claimed sixty-five lives over the course of nine days. On October 22, the Grand Trunk car ferry *Milwaukee* (3) sank with all hands in a gale while on a voyage between Milwaukee, Wisconsin and Grand Haven. While sources quote various figures, at least forty-seven perished in the sinking. Seven days later, the Goodrich steamer *Wisconsin* sank off Kenosha, Wisconsin with the loss of nine lives. Lastly, the Nicholson-Universal automobile carrier *Senator* (3) and Cleveland-Cliff's steamer *Marquette* (2) came together in a spectacular collision off Port Washington, Wisconsin on the fog-shrouded morning of October 31, 1929. Sinking within minutes, the former vessel took nine lives when it plunged to the bottom.[41]

With the wreck of the *Andaste* still awaiting discovery on the bottom of Lake Michigan, there is no way to determine the exact circumstances for its loss. Early in the search effort, Hugh P. Mulligan made a statement concerning this disaster that holds as true today as it did nearly 90 years ago. Pressed for information about the cause of the sinking, the steamboat inspector told news reporters, "Those who might tell the story, went down with the ship."[42]

NOTES

Chapter One
An Early Lake Superior Disappearance

1. John Brandt Mansfield, editor. *History of the Great Lakes, Volume I*. (Chicago, Illinois: J. H. Beers & Co., 1899), p. 197; Walter Havighurst. *The Long Ships Passing.* (New York City, New York: MacMillan Publishing Co., Inc., 1975), p. 161-162.
2. Sandusky Clarion, August 3, 1847; Walter Havighurst. *The Long Ships Passing.* (New York City, New York: MacMillan Publishing Co., Inc., 1975), p. 162-163.
3. Lewis Marvill. *First Trip by Steam to Lake Superior, Pioneer Collections, Report of the Pioneer Society of the State of Michigan, Volume IV.* (Lansing, Michigan: Wynkoop Hallenbeck Crawford Co., 1906), p. 67.
4. *Ibid.*, p. 68.
5. Ralph D. Williams. *The Honorable Peter White.* (Cleveland, Ohio: The Penton Publishing Company, 1905), p. 31-32.
6. Sandusky Clarion, August 3, 1847; Frederick Stonehouse. *Munising Shipwrecks.* (Au Train, Michigan: Avery Color Studios, 1983), p. 11.
7. Ralph D. Williams. *The Honorable Peter White.* (Cleveland, Ohio: The Penton Publishing Company, 1905), p. 32.
8. Sandusky Clarion, August 3, 1847.
9. Frederick Stonehouse. *Munising Shipwrecks.* (Au Train, Michigan: Avery Color Studios, 1983), p. 11.
10. *Ibid.*, p. 11; Buffalo Daily Republic, September 6, 1852.

Chapter Two
Missing for 150 Years

1. John B. Mansfield. *History of the Great Lakes, Volume 1.* (Chicago, Illinois: J. H. Beers & Company, 1899), p. 588.

2. John B. Mansfield. *History of the Great Lakes, Volume 1.* (Chicago, Illinois: J. H. Beers & Company, 1899), p. 598; James P. Barry. *Ships of the Great Lakes.* (Berkeley, California: Howell-North Books, 1973), p. 40-41; The *Clermont* was actually named *North River Steamboat.* The usage of *Clermont* in this passage is to reflect its more commonly known identity.

3. James P. Barry. *Ships of the Great Lakes.* (Berkeley, California: Howell-North Books, 1973), p. 52-53; John B. Mansfield. *History of the Great Lakes, Volume 1.* (Chicago, Illinois: J. H. Beers & Company, 1899), p. 403; John Ericsson became a United States citizen in 1848.

4. John B. Mansfield. *History of the Great Lakes, Volume 1.* (Chicago, Illinois: J. H. Beers & Company, 1899), p. 404.

5. John B. Mansfield. *History of the Great Lakes, Volume 1.* (Chicago, Illinois: J. H. Beers & Company, 1899), p. 444; Samuel P. Orth. *A History of Cleveland, Ohio, Volume 1.* (Cleveland, Ohio: The S.J. Clarke Publishing Co., 1910), p. 714.

6. John B. Mansfield. *History of the Great Lakes, Volume 2.* (Chicago, Illinois: J. H. Beers & Company, 1899), p. 22.

7. *Ibid.,* p. 22.

8. *Ibid.,* p. 22.

9. *Ibid.,* p. 51.

10. *Ibid.,* p. 23.

11. *Ibid.,* p. 23.

12. *Ibid.,* p. 23.

13. *Ibid.,* p. 23.

14. John B. Mansfield. *History of the Great Lakes, Volume 2.* (Chicago, Illinois: J. H. Beers & Company, 1899), p. 23; Oswego Times, November 4, 1862.

15. John B. Mansfield. *History of the Great Lakes, Volume 2.* (Chicago, Illinois: J. H. Beers & Company, 1899), p. 938.

16. The Oswego Times, November 4, 1862; Goderich Signal Semi-Weekly, November 14, 1862.

17. The Oswego Times, November 4, 1862; Goderich Signal Semi-Weekly, November 14, 1862; The Daily Sandusky Register, November 4, 1862.

18. The Janesville Daily Gazette, November 4, 1862; The Oswego Times, November 4, 1862.

19. The Oswego Times, November 4, 1862.
20. *Ibid.*
21. The Oswego Times, November 4, 1862; The Janesville Daily Gazette, November 4, 1862.
22. John B. Mansfield. *History of the Great Lakes, Volume 1.* (Chicago, Illinois: J. H. Beers & Company, 1899), p. 695.
23. The Blade, October 20, 2015; Syracuse Post-Standard, October 22, 2015.

Chapter Three
The Flying Dutchman of the Inland Seas

1. The Royal Center Record, April 30, 1897.
2. Manitoba Free Press, November 14, 1902.
3. Dwight Boyer. *Ghost Ships of the Great Lakes.* (New York City, New York: Dodd, Mead & Company, 1968), p. 17-18.
4. Manitoba Free Press, November 14, 1902.
5. Dwight Boyer. *Ghost Ships of the Great Lakes.* (New York City, New York: Dodd, Mead & Company, 1968), p. 17.
6. Julius F. Wolff, Jr. *Lake Superior Shipwrecks.* (Duluth, Minnesota: Lake Superior Port Cities, Inc., 1990), p. 98.
7. Alton Evening Telegraph, November 28, 1902.
8. Dwight Boyer. *Ghost Ships of the Great Lakes.* (New York City, New York: Dodd, Mead & Company, 1968), p. 19, 23; Julius F. Wolff, Jr. *Lake Superior Shipwrecks.* (Duluth, Minnesota: Lake Superior Port Cities, Inc., 1990), p. 98.
9. Dwight Boyer. *Ghost Ships of the Great Lakes.* (New York City, New York: Dodd, Mead & Company, 1968), p. 19.
10. The Burlington Hawk-Eye, November 29, 1902.
11. The Lowell Sun, November 29, 1902.
12. The Bradford Era, November 29, 1902; Dwight Boyer. *Ghost Ships of the Great Lakes.* (New York City, New York: Dodd, Mead & Company, 1968), p. 20-22.
13. Dwight Boyer. *Ghost Ships of the Great Lakes.* (New York City, New York: Dodd, Mead & Company, 1968), p.21; The Bradford Era, November 29, 1902.
14. Eau Claire Sunday Leader, November 30, 1902.
15. Dwight Boyer. *Ghost Ships of the Great Lakes.* (New York City, New York: Dodd, Mead & Company, 1968), p. 21-22.

16. Oakland Tribune, November 27, 1902.
17. Dwight Boyer. *Ghost Ships of the Great Lakes*. (New York City, New York: Dodd, Mead & Company, 1968), p.22; Alton Evening Telegraph, November 28, 1902.
18. Brainerd Daily Dispatch, November 28, 1902; Dwight Boyer. *Ghost Ships of the Great Lakes*. (New York City, New York: Dodd, Mead & Company, 1968), p. 23-24.
19. The Boston Globe, March 28, 1905; Some sources tell of a steel hull plate being found on the bottom of the Canadian Lock at Sault Ste. Marie, Ontario when it was drained at the end of the 1902 navigational season, thereby leading to some speculation it may have come from the *Bannockburn*.
20. Manitoba Morning Free Press, December 16, 1902.
21. Port Huron Daily Times, December 13, 1902; Julius F. Wolff, Jr. *Lake Superior Shipwrecks*. (Duluth, Minnesota: Lake Superior Port Cities, Inc., 1990), p. 98.; Manitoba Morning Free Press, December 16, 1902.
22. James Oliver Curwood. *The Great Lakes, The Vessels that Plough Them; Their Owners, Their Sailors, and Their Cargoes*. (New York City, New York: G. P. Putnam's Sons Great Lakes, 1909), p. 103; Frederick Stonehouse. *Went Missing Redux*. (Gwinn, Michigan: Avery Color Studios, Inc., 2008), p. 73.
23. Rodney Carlisle. *The Northern Mariner, Volume 17 No. 3, July 2007*. (Ottawa, Ontario: Canadian Nautical Research Society, 2007) p. 55-56.
24. Skip Gillham. *The Ships of Collingwood*. (St. Catharines, Ontario: Riverbank Traders, 1992), p. 5.
25. Marine Historical Society of Detroit, *Great Lakes Ships We Remember II*. (Cleveland, Ohio: Freshwater Press, Inc., 1984), p. 219.

Chapter Four
Lake Superior Claims Two More

1. The Evening News, April 14, 1905; John O. Greenwood. *The Fleet Histories Series, Volume 5*. (Cleveland, Ohio: Freshwater Press, Inc., 1998), p. 4.

2. John O. Greenwood. *Namesakes 1900-1909*. (Cleveland, Ohio: Freshwater Press, Inc., 1987), p. 210; Daily Times, May 19, 1894.
3. John O. Greenwood. *Namesakes 1900-1909*. (Cleveland, Ohio: Freshwater Press, Inc., 1987), p. 211.
4. The Logansport Journal, October 29, 1898; The Daily Northwestern, October 28, 1898; Some contemporary sources claim the *L. R. Doty* actually carried fifteen crewmembers.
5. The Logansport Journal, October 29, 1898; The Delphos Herald, October 28, 1898.
6. The Logansport Journal, October 29, 1898; The Republican Atlas, November 4, 1898.
7. The Logansport Journal, October 29, 1898.
8. The Marine Review, Volume 32 Number 10, September 7, 1905, p. 33.
9. Daily Crescent-News, September 6, 1905; The Marshall News, September 22, 1905; Julius F. Wolff, Jr. *Lake Superior Shipwrecks*. (Duluth, Minnesota: Lake Superior Port Cities, Inc., 1990), p. 109.
10. Julius F. Wolff, Jr. *Lake Superior Shipwrecks*. (Duluth, Minnesota: Lake Superior Port Cities, Inc., 1990), p. 105-107; Jasper Herald, September 8, 1905.
11. The Burlington Evening Gazette, September 7, 1905; Julius F. Wolff, Jr. *Lake Superior Shipwrecks*. (Duluth, Minnesota: Lake Superior Port Cities, Inc., 1990), p. 109.
12. Daily Crescent News, September 6, 1905; Jasper Herald, September 8, 1905; Julius F. Wolff, Jr. *Lake Superior Shipwrecks*. (Duluth, Minnesota: Lake Superior Port Cities, Inc., 1990), p. 109; The Marine Review, Volume 32 Number 10, September 7, 1905, p. 33.
13. Julius F. Wolff, Jr. *Lake Superior Shipwrecks*. (Duluth, Minnesota: Lake Superior Port Cities, Inc., 1990), p. 108.
14. Austin Daily Herald, September 6, 1905; Julius F. Wolff, Jr. *Lake Superior Shipwrecks*. (Duluth, Minnesota: Lake Superior Port Cities, Inc., 1990), p. 109.
15. Julius F. Wolff, Jr. *Lake Superior Shipwrecks*. (Duluth, Minnesota: Lake Superior Port Cities, Inc., 1990), p. 109; Austin Daily Herald, September 6, 1905; The Marine Review, Volume 32 Number 10, September 7, 1905, p. 33.

16. The Evening News, September 12, 1905.
17. The Evening News, September 12, 1905; The Daily Reflector, December 7, 1905.
18. The Evening News, September 12, 1905; Julius F. Wolff, Jr. *Lake Superior Shipwrecks*. (Duluth, Minnesota: Lake Superior Port Cities, Inc., 1990), p. 110.
19. The Evening News, September 12, 1905.
20. The Evening News, September 12, 1905; The Marshall News, September 22, 1905; Some sources claim the initials on the straps were actually "N.G.," which correspond to those of Nelson Gonyaw.
21. Julius F. Wolff, Jr. *Lake Superior Shipwrecks*. (Duluth, Minnesota: Lake Superior Port Cities, Inc., 1990), p. 109-110.
22. Julius F. Wolff, Jr. *Lake Superior Shipwrecks*. (Duluth, Minnesota: Lake Superior Port Cities, Inc., 1990), p. 109; Austin Daily Herald, September 6, 1905.
23. Julius F. Wolff, Jr. *Lake Superior Shipwrecks*. (Duluth, Minnesota: Lake Superior Port Cities, Inc., 1990), p. 107-108; John O. Greenwood. *Namesakes 1900-1909*. (Cleveland, Ohio: Freshwater Press, Inc., 1987), p. 118, 296.
24. Julius F. Wolff, Jr. *Lake Superior Shipwrecks*. (Duluth, Minnesota: Lake Superior Port Cities, Inc., 1990), p. 107; The Marine Review, Volume 32 Number 10, September 7, 1905, p. 33; Jasper Herald, September 8, 1905.
25. The Elkhart Review, September 9, 1905.

Chapter Five
Vanished From Sight

1. Daily British Whig, April 28, 1890.
2. *Ibid.*
3. John O. Greenwood. *Namesakes 1900-1909*. (Cleveland, Ohio: Freshwater Press, Inc., 1987), p. 340; John P. Barry. *Ships of the Great Lakes*. (Berkeley, California: Howell-North Books, 1973), p. 128-131.

4. John B. Mansfield. *History of the Great Lakes, Volume 1.* (Chicago, Illinois: J. H. Beers & Company, 1899), p. 503-504.
5. John P. Barry. *Ships of the Great Lakes.* (Berkeley, California: Howell-North Books, 1973), p. 171.
6. The Janesville Daily Gazette, October 23, 1905.
7. *Ibid.*
8. *Ibid.*
9. The Janesville Daily Gazette, October 23, 1905; The Bradford Era, October 21, 1905.
10. The Janesville Daily Gazette, October 23, 1905.
11. *Ibid.*
12. David D. Swayze. *Shipwreck!* (Boyne City, Michigan: Harbor House Publishers, 1992), p. 123; Logansport Daily Reporter, October 23, 1905; John O. Greenwood. *Namesakes 1910-1919.* (Cleveland, Ohio: Freshwater Press, Inc., 1986), p. 212.
13. The Bradford Era, October 21, 1905; John O. Greenwood. *Namesakes 1900-1909.* (Cleveland, Ohio: Freshwater Press, Inc., 1987), p. 48; John O. Greenwood. *Namesakes 1910-1919.* (Cleveland, Ohio: Freshwater Press, Inc., 1986), p. 500; John O. Greenwood. *Namesakes 1920-1929.* (Cleveland, Ohio: Freshwater Press, Inc., 1984), p. 325.
14. The Daily News, October 24, 1905; John O. Greenwood. *Namesakes 1900-1909.* (Cleveland, Ohio: Freshwater Press, Inc., 1987), p. 438.
15. Logansport Daily Reporter, October 23, 1905; The Bradford Era, October 21, 1905; David D. Swayze. *Shipwreck!* (Boyne City, Michigan: Harbor House Publishers, 1992), p. 217; John O. Greenwood. *Namesakes 1900-1909.* (Cleveland, Ohio: Freshwater Press, Inc., 1987), p. 104.
16. Logansport Daily Reporter, October 23, 1905; The Bradford Era, October 21, 1905; John O. Greenwood. *Namesakes 1900-1909.* (Cleveland, Ohio: Freshwater Press, Inc., 1987), p. 54, 174, 310; The Marine Review, Vol. 32 No. 17, October 26, 1905, p. 28.
17. The Janesville Daily Gazette, October 23, 1905.
18. The Evening News, October 27, 1905.
19. The Evening News, October 27, 1905; Manitoba Free Press, October 28, 1905.

20. Marine Historical Society of Detroit. *Great Lakes Ships We Remember III*. (Cleveland, Ohio: Freshwater Press, Inc., 1994), p. 405.

21. Sandusky Register, October 21, 1993; Chicago Tribune, October 21, 1993.

Chapter Six
Destined for Disaster

1. Julius F. Wolff, Jr. *Lake Superior Shipwrecks*. (Duluth, Minnesota: Lake Superior Port Cities, Inc., 1990), p. 107; The Marine Review, Volume 32 Number 10, September 7, 1905, p. 33; The Racine Daily Journal, September 5, 1905.

2. Lake Carriers' Association. *Annual Report of the Lake Carriers' Association 1950*. (Cleveland, Ohio: Lake Carriers' Association, 1951), p. 46; John O. Greenwood. *Namesakes 1900-1909*. (Cleveland, Ohio: Freshwater Press, Inc., 1987), p. 403; John F. Devendorf. *Great Lakes Bulk Carriers 1869-1985*. (Niles, Michigan: John F. Devendorf, 1996), p. 102.

3. Buffalo Evening News, April 14, 1906; The Marine Review, July 11, 1907, January 9, 1908.

4. The Marine Review, October 22, 1908, November 12, 1908, January 28, 1909; Many sources indicate that smoke from forest fires contributed to the grounding on Point Pelee.

5. The Marine Review, December 10, 1908; Julius F. Wolff, Jr. *Lake Superior Shipwrecks*. (Duluth, Minnesota: Lake Superior Port Cities, Inc., 1990), p. 128; The Marine Historical Society of Detroit, Inc. *Great Lakes Ships We Remember*. (Cleveland, Ohio: Freshwater Press, Inc., 1979), p. 136; The Evening News, December 7, 1908; Some sources list Duluth as the *Clemson*'s destination.

6. Julius F. Wolff, Jr. *Lake Superior Shipwrecks*. (Duluth, Minnesota: Lake Superior Port Cities, Inc., 1990), p. 128; The Evening News, December 8, 1908; The Marine Review, December 10, 1908; Captain F. D. Chamberlain of the *J. J.*

H. Brown apparently had no relation to Samuel R. Chamberlain of the *D. M. Clemson.*
7. The Evening News, December 15, 1908.
8. *Ibid.*, December 8, 1908.
9. Julius F. Wolff, Jr. *Lake Superior Shipwrecks.* (Duluth, Minnesota: Lake Superior Port Cities, Inc., 1990), p. 128; The Evening News, December 7, 1908, December 8, 1908; John O. Greenwood. *Namesakes 1910-1919.* (Cleveland, Ohio: Freshwater Press, Inc., 1986), p. 498.
10. The Evening Herald, December 7, 1908.
11. The Evening News, December 9, 1908; The Evening Herald, December 7, 1908.
12. The Marine Review, December 10, 1908; The Evening Herald, December 7, 1908; The Telegraph Herald, December 7, 1908.
13. The Evening News, 12-15-1908; John O. Greenwood. *Namesakes 1900-1909.* (Cleveland, Ohio: Freshwater Press, Inc., 1987), p. 343.
14. The Evening News, December 9, 1908.
15. The Evening News, December 8, 1908; The captain of the steamer *Palika* may have spotted the *Clemson* to the west of Whitefish Point.
16. The Evening News, December 8, 1908.
17. *Ibid.*, December 8, 1908.
18. *Ibid.*, December 9, 1908.
19. *Ibid.*, December 11, December 15, December 17, 1908.
20. *Ibid.*, December 11, 1908.
21. *Ibid.*, December 9, December 15, 1908.
22. *Ibid.*, December 10, 1908.
23. *Ibid.*, December 15, 1908.
24. Frederick Stonehouse. *Went Missing II.* (Au Train, Michigan: Avery Color Studios, 1984), p. 69.
25. Frederick Stonehouse. *Went Missing II.* (Au Train, Michigan: Avery Color Studios, 1984), p. 69; The Evening News, December 19, 1908.
26. The Evening News, December 19, 1908.
27. *Ibid.*, December 19, December 22, 1908.
28. *Ibid.*, December 22, 1908.
29. *Ibid.*, December 22, 1908.
30. *Ibid.*, December 19, December 22, 1908.

31. *Ibid.*, December 19, 1908.
32. *Ibid.*, December 22, 1908.
33. *Ibid.*, January 8, 1909.
34. Dwight Boyer. *Great Stories of the Great Lakes.* (New York City, New York: Dodd, Mead & Company, Inc., 1966), p. 85-86.
35. The Evening News, December 10, 1908; The Marine Historical Society of Detroit, Inc. *Great Lakes Ships We Remember.* (Cleveland, Ohio: Freshwater Press, Inc., 1979), p. 154.
36. The Evening News, December 15, 1908.
37. Escanaba Morning Press, May 29, 1909; The Evening News, May 18, 1909.
38. The Evening News, May 22, 1909.
39. The Marine Historical Society of Detroit, Inc. *Ahoy & Farewell II.* (Detroit, Michigan: The Marine Historical Society of Detroit, Inc., 1996), p. 64.

Chapter Seven
An Enduring Mystery

1. George W. Hilton. *The Great Lakes Car Ferries.* (Berkeley, California: Howell-North, 1962), 208-210; Dana Ashdown. *Railway Steamships of Ontario.* (Erin, Ontario: The Boston Mills Press, 1988), p. 154.
2. George W. Hilton. *The Great Lakes Car Ferries.* (Berkeley, California: Howell-North, 1962), p. 210-211.
3. John O. Greenwood. *Namesakes 1900-1909.* (Cleveland, Ohio: Freshwater Press, Inc., 1987), p. 315; George W. Hilton. *The Great Lakes Car Ferries.* (Berkeley, California: Howell-North, 1962), p. 202.
4. Conneaut News-Herald, December 10, 1909; Marine Historical Society of Detroit. *Great Lakes Ships We Remember II.* (Cleveland, Ohio: Freshwater Press, Inc., 1984), p. 51.
5. George W. Hilton. *The Great Lakes Car Ferries.* (Berkeley, California: Howell-North, 1962), p. 211.

6. Dwight Boyer. *Ghost Ships of the Great Lakes*. (New York City, New York: Dodd, Mead & Company, 1968), p. 150-151.
7. J. B. Mansfield. *History of the Great Lakes Volume II*. (Chicago, Illinois: J. H. Beers & Co., 1899), p. 697; Dwight Boyer. *Ghost Ships of the Great Lakes*. (New York City, New York: Dodd, Mead & Company, 1968), p. 145.
8. J. B. Mansfield. *History of the Great Lakes Volume II*. (Chicago, Illinois: J. H. Beers & Co., 1899), p. 697.
9. Ranging from 31 to 38, contemporary sources offer various numbers concerning the size of the vessel's crew when it departed on its final voyage. The 32 crewmembers quoted here is the most common figure provided by these accounts.
10. The Evening Herald, December 13, 1909.
11. Dwight Boyer. *Ghost Ships of the Great Lakes*. (New York City, New York: Dodd, Mead & Company, 1968), p. 151.
12. *Ibid.*, p. 152-153.
13. *Ibid.*, p. 156.
14. George W. Hilton. *The Great Lakes Car Ferries*. (Berkeley, California: Howell-North, 1962), p. 212; Dwight Boyer. *Ghost Ships of the Great Lakes*. (New York City, New York: Dodd, Mead & Company, 1968), p. 154; The steamer *Black* noted by several accounts of this shipwrecks is most likely the *Clarence A. Black* of the Pittsburgh Steamship Company.
15. Dwight Boyer. *Ghost Ships of the Great Lakes*. (New York City, New York: Dodd, Mead & Company, 1968), p. 155-156.
16. *Ibid.*, p. 157; The Washington Post, December 11, 1909.
17. The Evening Herald, December 11, 1909.
18. The Evening Herald, December 13, 1909; Dwight Boyer. *Ghost Ships of the Great Lakes*. (New York City, New York: Dodd, Mead & Company, 1968), p. 152.
19. The Evening Herald, December 13, 1909; Jay M. Osman. *Captain Jeremiah Driscoll and the Commodore Perry, Pennsylvania Angler & Boater, November/December 2001*. (Harrisburg, Pennsylvania: Commonwealth of Pennsylvania Fish and Boat Commission, 2001), p. 28.
20. The Evening Herald, December 13, 1909.

Notes

21. Skip Gillham. *Marquette & Bessemer No. 2*. (Port Huron,
    Michigan: The Times Herald); Jay M. Osman. *Captain
    Jeremiah Driscoll and the Commodore Perry, Pennsylvania
    Angler & Boate*r, *November/December 2001*. (Harrisburg,
    Pennsylvania: Commonwealth of Pennsylvania Fish and
    Boat Commission, 2001), p. 28.
22. Dwight Boyer. *Ghost Ships of the Great Lakes*. (New York
    City, New York: Dodd, Mead & Company, 1968), p. 163;
    The Evening Herald, December 13, 1909.
23. Skip Gillham. *Marquette & Bessemer No. 2*. (Port Huron,
    Michigan: The Times Herald); The Evening Herald,
    December 13, 1909.
24. Dwight Boyer. *Ghost Ships of the Great Lakes*. (New York
    City, New York: Dodd, Mead & Company, 1968), p. 164-
    165.
25. *Ibid.*, p. 167.
26. Dwight Boyer. *Ghost Ships of the Great Lakes*. (New York
    City, New York: Dodd, Mead & Company, 1968), p. 154;
    David D. Swayze. *Shipwreck!* (Boyne City, Michigan:
    Harbor House Publishers, Inc., 1992), p. 52, 201; John O.
    Greenwood. *Namesakes 1900-1909*. (Cleveland, Ohio:
    Freshwater Press, Inc., 1987), p. 6, 416; The Mansfield
    News, December 11, 1909.
27. The Logansport Chronicle, December 18, 1909.
28. The Logansport Daily Reporter, December 23, 1909; Dwight
    Boyer. *Ghost Ships of the Great Lakes*. (New York City,
    New York: Dodd, Mead & Company, 1968), p. 167.
29. Dwight Boyer. *Ghost Ships of the Great Lakes*. (New York
    City, New York: Dodd, Mead & Company, 1968), p. 160.
30. *Ibid.*, p. 160.
31. *Ibid.*, p. 158.
32. The Washington Post, December 11, 1909.
33. The Evening Record, April 7, 1910.
34. Dwight Boyer. *Ghost Ships of the Great Lakes*. (New York
    City, New York: Dodd, Mead & Company, 1968), p. 165.
35. Marine Historical Society of Detroit. *Great Lakes Ships We
    Remember*. (Cleveland, Ohio: Freshwater Press, Inc., 1979),
    p. 323; George W. Hilton. *The Great Lakes Car Ferries*.
    (Berkeley, California: Howell-North, 1962), p. 212-214.

168

36. Dwight Boyer. *Ghost Ships of the Great Lakes*. (New York City, New York: Dodd, Mead & Company, 1968), p. 164.
37. George W. Hilton. *The Great Lakes Car Ferries*. (Berkeley, California: Howell-North, 1962), p. 203, 215.
38. Marine Historical Society of Detroit. *Great Lakes Ships We Remember III*. (Cleveland, Ohio: Freshwater Press, Inc., 1994), p. 224; George W. Hilton. *The Great Lakes Car Ferries*. (Berkeley, California: Howell-North, 1962), p. 215; John O. Greenwood. *Namesakes 1956-1980*. (Cleveland, Ohio: Freshwater Press, Inc., 1981), p. 506.
39. Dwight Boyer. *Ghost Ships of the Great Lakes*. (New York City, New York: Dodd, Mead & Company, 1968), p. 168.

Chapter Eight
A Twin Disappearance

1. Following their 1970 merger, the communities of Fort William and Port Arthur became Thunder Bay, Ontario. Ships built on saltwater for Great Lakes service measuring too long to fit through the locks during this era were cut in two and rejoined after reaching a shipyard on the lakes. During World War I, several ships requisitioned for use on saltwater left the lakes in procedure opposite to the manner described here. Interestingly, the Port Arthur Shipbuilding Company in nearby Port Arthur built fourteen 125-foot naval trawlers for Canada's Department of Naval Services between 1917 and 1919.
2. The Marine Historical Society of Detroit, Inc. *Great Lakes Ships We Remember II*. (Cleveland, Ohio: Freshwater Press, Inc., 1984), p. 57.
3. Frederick Stonehouse. *Went Missing Redux*. (Gwinn, Michigan: Avery Color Studios, Inc., 2008), p. 120.
4. *Ibid*, p. 121.
5. *Ibid*, p. 138, 141-143.
6. Sheboygan Press, December 6, 1918.
7. Mark Bourrie. *Many a Midnight Ship*. (Ann Arbor, Michigan: The University of Michigan Press, 2005), p. 192.
8. Manitoba Free Press, December 4, 1918.

9. Julius F. Wolff, Jr. *Lake Superior Shipwrecks*. (Duluth, Minnesota: Lake Superior Port Cities, Inc., 1990), p. 160; Sheboygan Press, December 6, 1918.
10. Mark Bourrie. *Many a Midnight Ship*. (Ann Arbor, Michigan: The University of Michigan Press, 2005), p. 192.
11. The Brandon Daily Sun, December 6, 1918.
12. Manitoba Free Press, December 4, 1918; Frederick Stonehouse. *Went Missing Redux*. (Gwinn, Michigan: Avery Color Studios, Inc., 2008), p. 126; The Fort Wayne Journal-Gazette, December 6, 1918.
13. Frederick Stonehouse. *Went Missing Redux*. (Gwinn, Michigan: Avery Color Studios, Inc., 2008), p. 126-127.
14. The Evening Democrat, December 16, 1918. This newspaper account incorrectly reports Captain Leclerc as planning to leave Sault Ste. Marie, Michigan aboard the *Sebastopol*.

Chapter Nine
Sailed Away on Lake Erie

1. The Dunkirk Observer-Journal, April 11, 1889; Austin Daily Herald, March 29, 1897.
2. John B. Mansfield. *History of the Great Lakes, Volume 1*. (Chicago, Illinois: J. H. Beers & Company, 1899), p. 511.
3. The Waterloo Press, July 6, 1899.
4. The Burlington Evening Gazette, August 16, 1905; The Racine Daily Journal, August 16, 1905.
5. The Burlington Evening Gazette, August 16, 1905.
6. The Burlington Evening Gazette, August 16, 1905; The Racine Daily Journal, August 16, 1905.
7. The Burlington Evening Gazette, August 16, 1905.
8. *Ibid*.
9. The Burlington Evening Gazette, August 16, 1905; John O. Greenwood. *Namesakes 1910-1919*. (Cleveland, Ohio: Freshwater Press, Inc., 1986), p. 492.
10. The Syracuse Herald, December 29, 1922; Dwight Boyer. *Ghost Ships of the Great Lakes*. (New York City, New York: Dodd, Mead & Company, 1968), p. 192.

11. Syracuse Herald, January 2, 1923; Some sources indicate the *Cornell* was to enter the New York State Barge Canal via Oswego, New York. Such a voyage at this late date is impossible, however, as the Welland Canal closed for the season on December 14, 1922.
12. Syracuse Herald, December 27, 1922.
13. Dwight Boyer. *Ghost Ships of the Great Lakes.* (New York City, New York: Dodd, Mead & Company, 1968), p. 193; Lake Carriers' Association. *Annual Report of the Lake Carriers' Association, 1922.* (Cleveland, Ohio: Lake Carriers' Association, 1923), p. 201.
14. Syracuse Herald, December 27, 1922.
15. Syracuse Herald, December 27, 1922, January 2, 1923; Dwight Boyer. *Ghost Ships of the Great Lakes.* (New York City, New York: Dodd, Mead & Company, 1968), p. 193-194.
16. Syracuse Herald, December 27, 1922; The Sandusky Register, December 27, 1922.
17. Syracuse Herald, December 27, 1922; The Sandusky Register, December 27, 1922.
18. Syracuse Herald, June 26, 1922, December 29, 1922, January 6, 1923.
19. Syracuse Herald, December 27, 1922.
20. Syracuse Herald, January 2, 1923.
21. *Ibid.*
22. *Ibid.*
23. U.S. Department of Commerce. *Annual Report of the Supervising Inspector General, Steamboat Inspection Service to the Secretary of Commerce for the Fiscal Year Ended June 30, 1923.* (Washington D.C.: Department of Commerce, 1923), p. 15.

Chapter Ten
Doomed on Lake Michigan

1. Starke County Democrat, June 3, 1892.
2. John O. Greenwood. *The Fleet Histories Series, Volume 6.* (Cleveland, Ohio: Freshwater Press, Inc., 1998), p. 31-34.

3. *Ibid.*, p. 8, 34.
4. Port Arthur News, November 26, 1922.
5. John O. Greenwood. *The Fleet Histories Series, Volume 6.* (Cleveland, Ohio: Freshwater Press, Inc., 1998), p. 8; The Eau Claire Leader, July 25, 1923.
6. John O. Greenwood. *The Fleet Histories Series, Volume 6.* (Cleveland, Ohio: Freshwater Press, Inc., 1998), p. 8; Some sources refer to this company as the Cliffs-Leatham D. Smith Steamship Company.
7. The Lethbridge Herald, November 19, 1926.
8. The Herald-Palladium, October 7, 1976; Benjamin J. Shelak. *Shipwrecks of Lake Michigan.* (Black Earth, Wisconsin: Trails Books, 2003), p. 130.
9. John O. Greenwood. *The Fleet Histories Series, Volume 6.* (Cleveland, Ohio: Freshwater Press, Inc., 1998), p. 9.
10. *Ibid.*, p. 9.
11. *Ibid.*, p. 9.
12. Dwight Boyer. *Ghost Ships of the Great Lakes.* (New York City, New York: Dodd, Mead & Company, 1968), p. 65.
13. *Ibid.*, p. 72.
14. The News Palladium, September 16, 1929.
15. *Ibid.*
16. The Sandusky Register, September 14, 1929.
17. The Sandusky Register, September 14, 1929; Dwight Boyer. *Ghost Ships of the Great Lakes.* (New York City, New York: Dodd, Mead & Company, 1968), p. 67.
18. The News Palladium, September 16, 1929.
19. *Ibid.*
20. The Escanaba Daily Press, September 15, 1929.
21. The News Palladium, September 16, 1929.
22. The Escanaba Daily Press, September 17, 1929; Dwight Boyer. *Ghost Ships of the Great Lakes.* (New York City, New York: Dodd, Mead & Company, 1968), p. 68.
23. The News Palladium, September 16, 1929.
24. Dwight Boyer. *Ghost Ships of the Great Lakes.* (New York City, New York: Dodd, Mead & Company, 1968), p. 65-66; The Sandusky Register, September 14, 1929.
25. Dwight Boyer. *Ghost Ships of the Great Lakes.* (New York City, New York: Dodd, Mead & Company, 1968), p. 74.

26. The Herald-Palladium, October 7, 1976; The News Palladium, September 16, 1929.
27. Dwight Boyer. *Ghost Ships of the Great Lakes.* (New York City, New York: Dodd, Mead & Company, 1968), p. 66-67, 72.
28. The Escanaba Daily Press, September 13, 1929; The News-Palladium, September 10-12, 1929.
29. The News-Palladium, September 16, 1929.
30. The Escanaba Daily Press, September 15, 1929.
31. The News-Palladium, September 16, 1929.
32. Dwight Boyer. *Ghost Ships of the Great Lakes.* (New York City, New York: Dodd, Mead & Company, 1968), p. 69, 73-74.
33. The News-Palladium, September 13, 1929.
34. The Escanaba Daily Press, September 15, 17, 1929.
35. The Lewiston Daily Sun, September 16, 1929.
36. The News-Palladium, September 16, 1929.
37. Lebanon Daily News, September 17, 1929; Dwight Boyer. *Ghost Ships of the Great Lakes.* (New York City, New York: Dodd, Mead & Company, 1968), p. 69-71.
38. The Ludington Daily News, September 23, 1929; Dwight Boyer. *Ghost Ships of the Great Lakes.* (New York City, New York: Dodd, Mead & Company, 1968), p. 71, 77.
39. The News-Palladium, October 3, 1929; Dwight Boyer. *Ghost Ships of the Great Lakes.* (New York City, New York: Dodd, Mead & Company, 1968), p. 72-77.
40. The Escanaba Daily Press, July 6, 1929; The News-Palladium, September 16, 1929.
41. John O. Greenwood. *Namesakes 1920-1929.* (Cleveland, Ohio: Freshwater Press, Inc., 1984), p. 136, 138, 249.
42. The News-Palladium, September 16, 1929.

BIBLIOGRAPHY

Ashdown, Dana. *Railway Steamships of Ontario.* Erin, Ontario: The Boston Mills Press, 1988.

Bourrie, Mark. *Many a Midnight Ship.* Ann Arbor, Michigan: The University of Michigan Press, 2005.

Boyer, Dwight. *Ghost Ships of the Great Lakes.* New York City, New York: Dodd, Mead & Company, 1968.

———. *Great Stories of the Great Lakes.* New York City, New York: Dodd, Mead & Company, 1966.

Curwood, James Oliver. *The Great Lakes, The Vessels that Plough Them; Their Owners, Their Sailors, and Their Cargoes.* New York City, New York: G. P. Putnam's Sons Great Lakes, 1909.

Gillham, Skip. *The Ships of Collingwood.* St. Catharines, Ontario: Riverbank Traders, 1992.

Greenwood, John O. *Namesakes 1900-1909.* Cleveland, Ohio: Freshwater Press Inc., 1987.

———. *Namesakes 1910-1919.* Cleveland, Ohio: Freshwater Press Inc., 1986.

———. *Namesakes 1920-1929.* Cleveland, Ohio: Freshwater Press Inc., 1984.

———. *Namesakes 1956-1980.* Cleveland, Ohio: Freshwater Press Inc., 1981.

Havighurst, Walter. *The Long Ships Passing.* New York City, New York: MacMillan Publishing Co., Inc., 1975.

Hilton, George W. *The Great Lakes Car Ferries.* Berkeley, California: Howell-North, 1962.

Mansfield, John Brandt (Editor). *History of the Great Lakes, Volume I.* Chicago, Illinois: J. H. Beers & Co., 1899.

———. *History of the Great Lakes, Volume II.* Chicago, Illinois: J. H. Beers & Co., 1899.

Marine Historical Society of Detroit. *Great Lakes Ships We Remember.* Cleveland, Ohio: Freshwater Press, Inc., 1979.

———. *Great Lakes Ships We Remember II.* Cleveland, Ohio: Freshwater Press, Inc., 1984.

———. *Great Lakes Ships We Remember III.* Cleveland, Ohio: Freshwater Press, Inc., 1994.

Ratigan, William. *Great Lakes Shipwrecks and Survivals.* Grand Rapids, Michigan: Wm. B. Eerdmans Publishing Co., 1977.

Shelak, Benjamin J. *Shipwrecks of Lake Michigan.* Black Earth, Wisconsin: Trails Books, 2003.

Stonehouse, Frederick. *Went Missing – Redux.* Gwinn, Michigan: Avery Color Studios, Inc., 2008.

Swayze, David D. *Shipwreck!* Boyne City, Michigan: Harbor House Publishers, Inc., 1992.

Wolff, Julius F., Jr. *Lake Superior Shipwrecks.* Duluth, Minnesota: Lake Superior Port Cities, Inc., 1990.

Newspapers
Note: Related chapter numbers are in parenthesis. Some newspapers operated under various names throughout their publishing histories, thus some may appear more than once in this listing.

Alton, Illinois
Alton Evening Telegraph (3)

Benton Harbor, Michigan
News-Palladium (10)

Austin, Minnesota
Austin Daily Herald (4, 9)

Boston, Massachusetts
Boston Globe (3)

Bradford, Pennsylvania
Bradford Era (3, 5)

Brainerd, Minnesota
Brainerd Daily Dispatch (3)

Brandon, Manitoba
Brandon Daily Sun (8)

Buffalo, New York
Buffalo Daily Republic (1)
Buffalo Evening News (6)

Burlington, Iowa
Burlington Evening Gazette (4, 9)
Burlington Hawk-Eye (3)

Chicago, Illinois
Chicago Tribune (5)

Conneaut, Ohio
Conneaut News-Herald (7)

Defiance, Ohio
Daily Crescent-News (4)

Dubuque, Iowa
Telegraph Herald (6)

Dunkirk, New York
Dunkirk Observer-Journal (9)

Eau Clair, Wisconsin
Eau Claire Leader (10)
Eau Claire Sunday Leader (3)

Elkhart, Indiana
Elkhart Review (4)

Escanaba, Michigan
Escanaba Daily Press (10)
Escanaba Morning Press (6)

Fort Madison, Iowa
Evening Democrat (8)

Fort Wayne, Indiana
Fort Wayne Journal-Gazette (8)

Greenville, Pennsylvania
Evening Record (7)

Janesville, Wisconsin
Janesville Daily Gazette (2, 5)

Jasper, Indiana
Jasper Herald (4)

Kingston, Ontario
Daily British Whig (5)

Knox, Indiana
Starke County Democrat (10)

Lebanon, Pennsylvania
Lebanon Daily News (10)

Lethbridge, Alberta
Lethbridge Herald (10)

Lewiston, Maine
Lewiston Daily Sun (10)

Logansport, Indiana
Logansport Chronicle (7)
Logansport Daily Reporter (5, 7)
Logansport Journal (4)

Lowell, Massachusetts
Lowell Sun (3)

177

Ludington, Michigan
Ludington Daily News (10)

Marshall, Michigan
Daily News (5)
Marshall News (4)

Norwalk, Ohio
Evening Herald (6, 7)

Oakland, California
Oakland Tribune (3)

Oswego, New York
Oswego Times (2)

Port Arthur, Texas
Port Arthur News (10)

Port Huron, Michigan
Port Huron Daily Times (3)

Racine, Wisconsin
Racine Daily Journal (6, 9)

Royal Center, Indiana
Royal Center Record (3)

Sandusky, Ohio
Daily Sandusky Register (2)
Sandusky Clarion (1)
Sandusky Register (5, 9, 10)

Sault Ste. Marie, Michigan
Evening News (4, 5, 6)

Sheboygan, Wisconsin
Sheboygan Press (8)

St. Joseph, Michigan
Herald-Palladium (10)

Syracuse, New York
Post-Standard (2)
Syracuse Herald (9)

Toledo, Ohio
The Blade (2)

Washington, D.C.
Washington Post (7)

Waterloo, Indiana
Waterloo Press (9)

Winnipeg, Manitoba
Manitoba Free Press (3, 5, 8)
Manitoba Morning Free Press (3)

INDEX

187